William Graham Sumner

Problems in Political Economy

William Graham Sumner

Problems in Political Economy

ISBN/EAN: 9783744645201

Printed in Europe, USA, Canada, Australia, Japan

Cover: Foto ©Suzi / pixelio.de

More available books at **www.hansebooks.com**

PROBLEMS

IN

POLITICAL ECONOMY

By

WILLIAM GRAHAM SUMNER

Professor of Political and Social Science in Yale College

NEW YORK
HENRY HOLT AND COMPANY
1889

CONTENTS.

PREFACE.

When I began to make this collection of problems I intended to make only a small pamphlet for use in my own class-room. The enterprise has grown, however, until it has seemed better to make a book and publish it. Hence a few words of explanation are here needed.

I have long used problems and fallacies as auxiliary to my other class-room work. The object of such exercises is to break up the routine of text-book recitations, to encourage wider study of scientific treatises, and to develop some independent power of thinking, and of applying the principles which have been learned. In the present state of political economy it seems especially desirable to study subjects, and not text-books. These problems are intended to bring forward the subjects or topics which should be studied, and to guide the student to an investigation of them with the aid of the teacher, and by the use of the leading treatises in the science. The problems are, in their form, almost all " leading," and effort has been made to put them in such a way that a student who has already studied an elementary text-book can deal with them. When possible, they have been put in that form in which they present themselves in practice. My aim has been to limit the references as much as possible in number, and to concentrate them on the following books: Rogers's Adam Smith, Mill's Principles, Jevons' Theory, Marshall's Economics of Industry, Cairnes's Principles, Walker's Political Economy, and Cossa's Guide. A " Loan Library of Political Economy" has been formed as a part of the scheme, from which each student can obtain a copy of each of the above books for use so long as he desires. I have found, however, that, if the problems were to have any range and variety, I must enlarge the range of the references far beyond my original intention. I give below a list of all the books to which reference is made under the problems. The library will contain these in numbers proportioned to their usefulness.

While I was at work on these problems Milnes' collection of 2,000 questions and problems from English examination papers was published. I have to acknowledge my obligations to that collection. I have borrowed some problems from it; others I have adapted. They are marked by an M. with the number in Milnes' collection, thus: (M. 100). Many have been suggested to me by reading that collection. I have given credit whenever the suggestion was so close that I could specify the question in Milnes' collection which suggested mine. This was not always possible, and so the present general acknowledgment must cover the rest.

The problems here given are of very unequal difficulty and importance. A primary classification is made by printing the numbers of those which I should reserve for examination at a later stage of study with thin faced numerals.

I am indebted to Prof. H. W. Farnam and Mr. Arthur Hadley for valuable aid and suggestions.

W. G. S.

YALE COLLEGE, December, 1883.

FULL TITLES OF BOOKS CITED.

Accounts and Papers, Session [Parliament] 1868-9, vol. 35, (Public Finances since 1688).

Baden-Powell, State Aid and State Interference. Chapman & Hall, 1882.

Bagehot, Lombard Street. Scribner, Armstrong & Co., 1873.

Banker's Magazine. New York.

Brodrick, English Land and English Landlords. Cassel & Co., 1881.

Cairnes, Logical Method of Political Economy. Macmillan, 1875.

Cairnes, Some Principles of Political Economy. Harpers.

Cairnes, Essays in Political Economy, Theoretical and Applied. Macmillan, 1873.

Chevalier, *Économie Politique*. Paris, 1866.

Chevalier, On Gold (Translated). Appleton, 1859.

Cossa, Guide to the Study of Political Economy (Translated). Macmillan, 1880.

Crump, English Manual of Banking. Longmans, 1877.

Cunningham, Growth of English Industry and Commerce. Cambridge, University Press, 1882.

DeBroglie, *Le Libre Échange et L'Impot.* Paris, 1879.

DeLavelaye, Primitive Property (Translated). Macmillan, 1878.

Dictionnaire de l'Économie Politique. Guillaumin, 1854.

Fawcett, Political Economy, 6th Ed. Macmillan, 1883.

Fawcett, Pauperism. Macmillan, 1871.

Fawcett, Free Trade and Protection. Macmillan, 1878.

Ford, American Citizen's Manual. Putnam, 1883.

Giffen, Essays in Finance. Geo. Bell & Sons, 1880.

Gilbart, The Principles and Practice of Banking. Bell & Daldy, 1871.

viii

Goschen, Theory of the Foreign Exchanges.　E. Wilson, 1875.

Grant, Recess Studies.　Edmonston & Douglas, Edinburgh, 1870.

Hankey, The Principles of Banking.　Effingham Wilson, 1873.

Hertzka, *Währung und Handel*.　Wien, 1876.

Holyoake, History of Coöperation in England.　Lippincott, 1875.

Horton, Silver and Gold.　R. Clarke & Co., 1876.

Humboldt, Sphere and Duties of Government.　London, 1854.

Hamilton. National Debt of Great Britain.　Carey, 1816.

Jevons, Theory of Political Economy.　Macmillan, 1879.

Jevons, Money and the Mechanism of Exchange.　Appleton, 1875.

Jevons, The Coal Question.　Macmillan, 1866.

Jevons, Methods of Social Reform.　Macmillan, 1883.

Lalor, Cyclopedia of Political Science, etc.　Rand, McNally & Co., 1882.

Leroy-Beaulieu, *Science des Finances*.　Guillaumin, 1877.

Letourneau, Sociology (Translated).　Chapman & Hall, 1881.

Levi, History of British Commerce.　Murray, 1880.

Macleod, Principles of Economical Philosophy.　Longmans. 1872.

Macleod, Dictionary of Political Economy.　Longmans, 1863.

Maine, Village Communities.　Holt, 1871.

Mann, Paper Money.　Appleton, 1872.

Marshall, Economics of Industry.　Macmillan, 1879.

Martineau, History of England.　Boston, 1865.

McCulloch's Adam Smith.　Longmans, 1838.

Mill, Political Economy.　Longmans, 1878.

Mill, Logic.　Harpers, 1870.

Mill, Liberty.　Longmans, 1865.

Milnes, Problems in Political Economy.　Sonnenschein, 1882.

Molesworth, History of England.　Chapman & Hall, 1874.

Mongredien, History of the Free Trade Movement in England. Cassell & Co.

Mongredien, Wealth Creation.　Cassell & Co., 1882.

Price, Practical Political Economy.　Kegan Paul & Co., 1878.

Princeton Review, November, 1879, Bimetalism.

Princeton Review, March, 1881, The Argument Against Protective Taxes.

Princeton Review, November, 1881, Sociology.

Princeton Review, November, 1882, Wages.
Probyn, Systems of Land Tenure in Various Countries. Cassell & Co.
Ricardo, Works, Edited by McCulloch. Murray, 1881.
Richardson, H. A., National Banks. Harpers.
Richardson, W. A., Public Debt and National Banking Laws of the United States. Washington, 1873.
Rogers, History of Agriculture and Prices in England. Clarendon Press, 1866.
Roscher, Political Economy (translated). Holt, 1878.
Say, *Rapport sur le Payement de l'Indemnité de Guerre*, in his Translation of Goschen, *Theorie des Changes*. Guillaumin, 1875.
Seebohm, The English Village Community. Longmans, 1883.
Seybert, Statistical Annals. Philadelphia, 1818.
Seyd on Bullion and Foreign Exchanges. Effingham Wilson, 1868.
Sidgwick, Principles of Political Economy. Macmillan, 1883.
Smith, Adam, Wealth of Nations, edited by Rogers. Clarendon Press, 1880.
Smith, Adam, edited by McCulloch, see McCulloch.
Soetbeer, *Petermann's Mittheilungen, Ergänzungsheft, Nr. 57, Edelmetall-produktion.* Gotha, 1879.
Spencer, Study of Sociology. Appleton, 1874.
Spencer, Principles of Sociology. Appleton, 1883.
Spencer, Biology. Appleton. 1874.
Spencer, Social Statics. Appleton, 1863.
Spencer, Essays, Moral, Political and Esthetic. Appleton, 1872.
Sumner, Life of Jackson. Houghton, Mifflin & Co., 1882.
Sumner, Argument before the Tariff Commission, 1882.
Sumner, History of Protection in the United States. Putnam.
Sumner, What Social Classes Owe to Each Other. Harpers, 1883.
Sumner, see " Princeton Review."
Thornton, On Labor. Macmillan, 1870.
Walker, Political Economy. Holt, 1883.
Walker, Money. Holt, 1878.
Walker, Money, Trade and Industry. Holt, 1879.

Walker, Land and its Rent. Little & Brown, 1883.

Wallace, Russia. Holt, 1877.

Walras, *Éléments d' Économie Politique Pure.* Lausanne, 1874.

Ward, Dynamic Sociology. Appleton, 1883.

Wilson, The National Budget. Macmillan, 1882.

Woolsey, Political Science ; or, The State. Scribner, Armstrong
& Co., 1878.

ADDED 1885.

Connell, The Economic Revolution of India. Kegan Paul, 1883.

Frohme, *Die Entwickelung der Eigenthumsverhältnisse.* Bocken-
heim, 1883.

Le Touzé, *Traité du Change.* Guillaumin, 1883.

Le Play. *La Reforme Sociale en France.* Dentu, 1878.

Pollock, The Land Laws. Macmillan, 1883.

Rae, Contemporary Socialism. Scribners, 1884.

Rogers, Work and Wages. Putnams, 1884.

Taylor, Profit-sharing. Kegan Paul, 1884.

ECONOMIC PROBLEMS.

1.

GENERAL DEFINITIONS.

1. Discuss the following definitions of political economy: It is the science of value.

It is the science of exchanges.

It is the science which treats of the production, exchange and distribution of wealth.

Political economy, or economics, is the name of that body of knowledge which relates to wealth.

Political economy is the science which investigates the laws of the material welfare of human societies.

Cairnes, Logical Method, 57.

2. Is political economy not a science (1) because, as is alleged, it cannot predict economic phenomena; (2) because, as is alleged, it has not won a body of positive and ascertained results? What is a science? or what is the essential condition that any discipline may become a science?

Marshall, 2.

3. Sociology is the science of life in society. Political economy is that branch of sociology which treats of the industrial organization of society. Expand the notion and definition of sociology and explain what that conception of political economy is which is here presented.

4. Price says that it is silly to call political economy a science; that supply and demand, the law of population, etc., are only familiar facts of intelligent observation. *Per contra*, he affirms that political economy is "the application of common sense to familiar processes. It explains their nature and manner of working. It analyzes and thinks out practices which are universal except when thwarted by artificial theory."—Criticise this view of political economy as antithetical to the notion of a science. What is it to think out a practice? What is a practice which would be universal, if not thwarted? What is an artificial theory? How can a theory thwart a practice?
Price, 10–15.

5. Wealth is any material good which satisfies a desire of man, and which is not gratuitous. It is used as a collective term, for the general conception of such goods, and, when it describes the subject or aim of political economy, it carries with it the notion of abundance.—Criticise and

correct this definition. Do you include in your definition the following? Honesty, health, skill, "the moral, intellectual, and physical natures" of the people, a patent right, a copy-right, a bill of exchange, the voice of a singer, a good harbor, climate, and sunlight. Do you infer, for instance from Price's discussion, that economists need *not* continue the effort to formulate a satisfactory definition of wealth?

Price, 23–30.   Marshall, 6.   Sidgwick, Chap. III.
Adam Smith, I., 1, Rogers's note.

6. If a census were taken of the wealth of the country ought the owners of land to return it at its market value? Is the land a part of the national wealth? Ought the owners of government bonds to include them in the return? If they did so, and if the returns were added up, the national debt would be counted into the sum of the national wealth. Would that be right? If A sells to B a bale of cotton for $500 and B gives a promissory note for it, ought B to return the cotton and A the note? If A has a certificate of stock in a railroad, ought the railroad officers to return the railroad and ought A to return the stock?

Adam Smith, I., 254, Rogers's note.

7. "Because political economy confines itself to discovering the laws of wealth, it has, by some,

been called derisively, the gospel of mammon.
In reply to this sneer it would be enough to say
that, while wealth is not the sole interest of man-
kind, perhaps not the highest interest, it is yet of
vast concern, of vital concern to individuals and
to communities.   As such it deserves to be
studied.   Now, if it is to be studied at all, it will
best be studied by itself."—Vindicate in detail
this view of political economy and show the relation of political economy to other interests.
    Walker, Pol. Ec., I, 2.

8. If there should be a scarcity of houses in the
city of Washington this winter, would that fact
constitute a problem requiring the attention of
the economists of the country?   How does your
answer bear on the sphere of political economy
and the opinions of the professorial socialists?

9. It has been said that the free play of economic forces would produce, not the best conceivable, but the worst conceivable, state of
society.   Show the absurdity of this statement.

10. What are economic forces?   What are
economic laws?   Are economic laws subject to
exceptions—like laws of grammar?   Are economic laws like the ten commandments?   Are
they like Acts of Congress?   Are they like laws

of physics? Can we "violate" them? What is the limit of what we can do with economic forces? If economic laws are described as expressing a "tendency," what is meant? What objection is there to that description of them?

Marshall, 3.   Cairnes, Logical Method, 18.

Cairnes, Principles, 184.   Mill's Logic, Book III., Chap. 10, §5.

Cossa, 7.   Sidgwick, 24.   Spencer, Study of Sociology, 22.

11. A writer who ridicules the notion of natural or scientific laws in political economy cites "property" as a proof that no such laws exist. Show the fallacy.

12. Distinguish between the science and art of political economy; between political economy and politics.

Walker, Pol. Econ., 20–22.   Cossa, 6, 11–13.

13. Is it a valid distinction to say that the science of political economy investigates what is; the art, what ought to be?

Sidgwick, 23–26, also 402.

14. Does the art of political economy mean, or include, the art of getting rich, or the art of conducting business, or the art of speculation, or the art of investing capital in stocks, bonds, lands, etc., or the art of conducting the finances of a nation, or the art of legislating on trade, in-

dustry, and finance? Give reasons for including
or excluding each of these things.

15. Is political economy a "moral" science?
If so, according to what classification of the
sciences is it so classed? and what is meant by so
denominating it?
Cairnes, Logical Method, 31, 37.

16. Is political economy a deductive or an in-
ductive science? What difference does it make
which it is
Cairnes, Logical Method, 60 fg.   Sidgwick, Chap. III.

17. Is imagination a force in political economy? If so, give all the illustrations you can.
Discuss delusion, fraud, falsehood, prejudice,
habit, tradition, patriotism and affection, so far
as you think that an economist ought to take
account of them.

Ought there to be any difference in a text-
book of political economy for an English college
and for a college in India?
Walker, Polit. Econ., 23.
Connell, 11–22; 50; 148–9.

18. If it is said: "Some people struggle to
keep up false appearances of wealth and so ruin
themselves," do you think that that is such an
observation as an economist should take account
of? If it is said: "Many people waste their capi-

tal by extravagant expenditure," do you think that that is an observation of which an economist should take account?

19. Do you think, as a matter of fact, that most people actually distribute their incomes in their expenditure so as to get the maximum of utility for themselves, judging by such standards of utility as they would admit to be sound when discussing the question of what things are useful abstractly? If there are many who do not do so, does that present a fact which the economist ought to take note of in his discussions?
Jevons, Theory, 77–80; 149–153.

20. Do you believe that there are crafty and able men who can "rig the market" and bull and bear prices more or less at their pleasure? Mention commodities with which this might be more possible than with others. Is it possible with stocks? If so, why? What should you say of such interferences on the whole and over a considerable period of time? Is the popular opinion correct about the extent to which manipulation of the market is possible?
Banker's Magazine, XXXVI., 308.

21. Was it the fundamental doctrine of the mercantile system that the precious metals are

wealth exclusively or preëminently?   If not,
what was the fundamental doctrine of that system, and how was the doctrine just mentioned
derived from it?   Describe the development of
the system.

Adam Smith, I., 15, Rogers's note ; II., 63, Rogers's note.
Cossa, 119, fg.

22. How was the colonial system a deduction
from the mercantile system?

Adam Smith, II., 190–210.

23. Who were the Physiocrats and what did
they teach?

Cossa, 142.   Art. *Physiocrates* in the *Dictionnaire de l'Ec. Pol.*

24. Mention the leading English economists
from Smith to J. S. Mill, giving dates and the
chief contributions of each.

Cossa, 161–182.   Life of Smith prefaced to Rogers's Smith.

II.

ELEMENTARY PRINCIPLES.

25. What is meant by a period of production? Show the great importance of observing the element of time in economic phenomena and correctly defining it in economic generalizations.

Jevons, Theory, 249–258.

26. What could supply and demand mean to Robinson Crusoe? When, in history, did supply and demand begin to act?

Supply and demand, at their lowest terms, are not a ratio, but a case of two simultaneous equations between two variables, or, they are represented by two curves which intersect. There are two .persons and two commodities.—Prove this and show what errors must follow from treating supply and demand as a simple ratio.

How far can we analyze supply and demand?

Is the equilibrium of supply and demand accidental, imperfect, arbitrary, contingent, moral, or mathematical?

Jevons, Theory, Chap. IV.
Jenkin in Grant's Recess Studies, 151–171.
Princeton Review, November, 1882, p. 249–50

27. Effort and satisfaction are the pulsations by which the isolated man maintains existence. So soon as society exists division of labor begins and exchange follows. The systole and diastole of supply and demand are the form which the pulsations of effort and satisfaction take for a man who lives in society. Hence supply and demand are constant and all-pervading relations in society, and demand the first and most careful study of the economist.

Rights and obligations are the jurisprudential aspect of the relations of supply and demand.— Expand and criticise.

28. The law of supply and demand, in a free market without reserve, is that they come to an equilibrium at the ratio of value which will clear the market.—Compare Mill's law of the equation of international value and criticise the law here stated.

Mill, III., 18, §4.

29. What is the difference between supply and demand and reciprocal demand?

Mill, III., 18, §4.   Cairnes, Principles, 89.

30. Value is a fact, not an opinion. It therefore has conditions of time and place, and may vary from moment to moment or place to place if successive sales take place.—Expand, illustrate, and establish, or refute, this statement.

31. "Value, economists are pretty much agreed, is a relation; and, for the purposes of the present discussion, we may so take it." A few pages further on: "Value is purchasing power; power in exchange." What further analysis is necessary to make these two definitions consistent?
Walker, Money and Trade, 30, 36.

32. "Wheat is worth 24 francs the hectolitre. This fact has the character of a natural fact. This value of wheat, reckoned in silver, does not result either from the will of the seller, or the will of the buyer, or from an agreement between them." "Wheat is worth 24 francs the hectolitre. This is a mathematical fact. The value of wheat in silver yesterday was 22 or 23 francs. A little while ago it was 23½ or 23¾. It will shortly be 24¼ or 24½. But to-day, at this instant, it is 24 francs, neither more nor less. This is a mathematical fact and admits of mathematical expression."—Explain and prove.
Walras, 29, 30.

33. If the supply of all commodities were doubled or halved suddenly, would any changes in their relative value ensue or not? (M. 774.)
Jevons, Theory, 160–174.   Mill, IV., 3, §4.

34. On the Black Friday of 1869 gold was sold on one side of the gold room for 160 when it was being sold on the other side for 135. Those on one side of the room knew a minute sooner than those on the other side that the Secretary of the Treasury had ordered five million dollars gold to be sold, adding so much to the supply.— How does this illustrate the doctrine of value? Cf. question 30.

35. Is either one of the following things commensurable ; if so, which? Cost, desire, utility, satisfaction. What is "cost" according to Cairnes?

Cairnes, Principles, 73–87.

36. Why does not skill enter into cost? Is the fact here analogous to the fact that the rent of land does not enter into the price of agricultural produce?

Cairnes, Principles, 76–80.

37. Translate into English, *prix de revient.*

38. It is commonly said that value, in the long run, conforms to "cost of production." Jevons says : "I hold labor to be essentially variable, so that its value must be determined by the value

of the produce, not the value of the produce by that of labor." "Labor once spent has no influence on the future value of any article." He defines labor "all exertion of body or mind" by which we get products, and he says that it is incommensurable. Cairnes defines "cost" as all onerous exertion and sacrifice necessary to get goods. Macleod denies that labor produces value. He says that value produces or calls out labor. Sidgwick objects to Cairnes's use of "cost" that Cairnes spoke of the proportion of cost of production, but that we cannot think of "anything being in proportion to an aggregate of incommensurables." Marshall recognizes two uses of cost of production, adopts Cairnes's notion, and proposes the term "expenses of production" for the outlay, to which, as he and others say, normal value must conform.—Is Sidgwick's objection valid? Compare the above views and say whether the two senses of cost of production should be recognized, or, if only one, which?

Mill, III., ch. 3.   Jevons, Theory, 174–18p.
Sidgwick, 201.   Macleod, Econ. Philos., I., 331.

39. Jevons says that "Labor once spent has no influence on the future value of any article." On the wages system, if the labor spent last week was paid for by capital then consumed by

the laborer, can value to be received ever have
any effect back upon labor expended? or value
be made to conform to capital formerly laid out?
If we say that we shall make a new adjustment,
in the next period of production, if we fail to replace our capital, will not the next period of
production have all its own facts, circumstances
and relations, and be, in fact, a new and independent problem?

40. Cost of production is a comparison of
ratios. Cost is incommensurable, but the subject
of it compares the cost with the satisfaction
obtained. This ratio he cannot measure. It
could not be measured and compared for two
men, but the first man can compare the cost to
him and the satisfaction to him in one line with
the cost to him and the satisfaction to him in
another, and this is what is really essential and is
really done so long as two or more lines are
open. Hence cost of production redistributes
labor and capital and acts on supply; so ulti-
mately on value. In no other way does it act on
value, which is controlled by supply and demand
only.—Criticise this doctrine. Suppose that no
second line is open, and that the ratio of satisfaction to effort falls, as when a laborer advanced in
life has to compete with a machine which lowers
the price of his product, what happens then? and

what becomes of the notion of cost of production as an ultimate regulator of value? What light does this last supposition throw on the last two questions?

41. "All other organs, therefore, jointly and individually, compete for blood with each organ, so that, though the welfare of each is indirectly bound up with that of the rest, yet, directly, each is antagonistic to the rest." " Evidently this process [of enlargement of an industry or development of a district whose products are in unusual demand] in each social organ, as in each individual organ, results from the tendency of the units to absorb all they can from the common stock of materials for sustentation ; and evidently the resulting competition, not between units simply, but between organs, causes in a society, as in a living body, high nutrition and growth of parts called into greatest activity by the requirements of the rest."

Explain the doctrine of the first sentence and show how it applies to society. What light is here thrown on competition as a mode of growth, and on the general laws of life of which competition is one phase?

Spencer's Principles of Sociology, I., 535-6,

42. Criticise the expression "division of labor." Explain social organization. Show that division of labor is only a case of it. Show the power and utility of organization. What is proved in regard to the social and industrial utility of concord and peace? What is the law of the " Increasing Return?"

Marshall, Chap. VII., p. 57.

43. "Are the following to be included in capital? (1) the original powers of the laborer; (2) his acquired powers; (3) the original properties of the soil; (4) improvements on land; (5) credit; (6) unsold stock in the hands of a merchant; (7) articles purchased but still in the consumer's hands." (M. 166.)

Jevons, Theory, 280–8.   Sidgwick, 120–141.

44. The savings of the United States have been estimated at 850 millions of dollars a year. What sort of things are these savings and where are they? (M. 177.)

Price, 113-14.   Marshall, 15.

45. Capital is transmuted in every period of production. Prove this. Show its relation to " risk," and to any sound doctrine of wages.

Show that industry is limited by capital.

Mill, I., 5, §§1, 3, 5.

46. The socialists declare that capital is produced (1) by accumulating the differences between buying price and selling price, i. e. the profits of merchants, and (2) by accumulating the differences between product and capital distributed to laborers. They regard the product as due entirely to labor, and therefore denounce the latter difference as an abstraction from the laborer of what belongs to him. They therefore construe the history of the last five hundred years as a period in which the middle class has developed itself by the accumulation of capital, (i. e. the plunder of the proletariat) and the creation of a capitalist system of industry. They construe civil liberty as the license given by the state to the robbery mentioned, and denounce competition as the mode in which the robbery is accomplished.

State what facts in the industrial history of the last five hundred years are here misconstrued, show the misconstruction, and put the facts in their true light.

Give an outline of the history of capital. When did it begin to be?

Describe the modern industrial system as compared with the system in England in the thirteenth century.

Cunningham, especially 139, 249. Seebohm.
Adam Smith, I., 273, Rogers's note. Walker, Land, 188.
Rogers, Work and Wages. Frohme. Rae, ch. III.

47. Mention as many natural monopolies as you can. State when and why space, light, air, and water have value. Do honesty and truth have value? If so, why? Are natural monopolies beneficent or maleficent to man? Illustrate.

48. If fresh meat has hitherto been wasted in Australia and Buenos Ayres, and if refrigerator ships can be constructed which can carry that meat to Europe, what effects can you trace on the prices of certain commodities, on the distribution and increase of population, and on international competition in industry as likely to be produced?
Adam Smith, I., 245.

49. What is a speculator? Is he a parasite on the commercial system? If he performs a service, what is it? Is it a correct definition to say that he is one who bets on variations in prices?
Cairnes, Principles, 109.   Adam Smith, II., 89 note ; 99.
Nation, VII., 85.

50. Can we ever become too rich? Has the work to be done any limits? Is the work to be done a positive quantity? Does it remain constant?
Cairnes, Principles, 249–262.

51. "As the washing of clothes is not a productive industry, and its cost is one of the charges of living, it is an object that it should occasion as little drain upon the pecuniary resources of the community as possible."
Criticise the distinction between productive and unproductive labor.

52. Would it be a good state of things if no man could be found who would black another man's shoes for less than a dollar? Suppose, first, that all were proud and shiftless, and then make other suppositions.

53. " Discuss ·the effects of the exportation of capital (1) from England, (2) from Ireland." (M. 219.)

54. Can you assign any meaning to " over-production" in any case whatever.
Jevons, Theory, 219–221.

55. A cause of industrial depression was said to be " that the power to consume has not kept pace with the power to produce. It is not the fault of the power of production, [i. e., it is not over production.] It is a fault on the other side."

If production should exceed consumption, what would become of the difference?   If consumption should exceed production, where would we get the difference?

Cairnes, Principles, 31–36.

56. What are the economic objections to gambling?

Cf. Jevons, 172–174.   Spencer, Study of Sociology, 306.

57. In a certain city a piece of grading was to be done.   It was known and admitted that it would cost 15 cents per cubic foot to do it by contract and 45 cents per foot to do it by days labor.   Some favored doing it the latter way and replied to the objection of greater cost that there would be no loss or injury to the interest of the city because the money would be paid to laborers resident in the city, and so would stay there.— Show the fallacy of this reasoning.

58. Suppose that, in consequence of great reduction in the cost of transportation between the United States and England, the gains of agriculture in England should greatly decline, what would be the successive stages of effect, and what the ultimate effect on the wealth of England, and why?   (M. 38.)   What would be the effect in the United States?

59. What is the value of the obelisk in the Central Park? Its first cost to its modern owner was o. It cost $100,000 to move it and set it up.
Jevons, Theory, 174-180.

60. A one dollar bank note is in circulation, which is a counterfeit, but no one has detected it. What is its value?

The promoters of a stock company, by puffing it in the newspapers, have run the stock up to 150. What is the value of it?

A false bottom was put into an elevator bin so that it held 50 bushels when it was supposed to hold 10,000. What was the effect on the market price of wheat? What was the value of wheat?

A piece of cloth was sold for all wool for $1.00 a yard. It contained 10 per cent. cotton. What was its value?

A grocer tampered with his scales so that he sold 15 ounces for a pound. He charged " 10 cts. a pound" for sugar. What was the value of sugar?

61. A piece of land was owned by 15 persons. Desiring to divide without selling it, they employed three real estate experts to divide it into 15 parts which should be of equal value. This was done. The next year the tax assessors assessed the 15 shares at amounts varying from $900 to $2,850.

What light does this incident throw on value?

62. In 1870 a house was built which cost $100,000. In 1876 it was appraised in an estate at $75,000 because that was judged to be what it would sell for. In 1880 it was sold for $150,000. There were those who claimed in 1876 that it should be appraised at what it cost in 1870, or at what it would sell for in 1880 so far as they could then foresee that. What do you say?

63. What causes determine the market value of oysters?

Cairnes, Principles, 141–146.

64. "Suppose a considerable rise in the price of wool to be foreseen, how should farmers expect the prices of mutton, beef and hides, respectively to be affected, and why?" (M. 868.)

65. The Dutch East India Co. used to destroy part of the spice crop in order to enhance its profits. Was there a fallacy in the proceeding? (M. 547.)

Adam Smith, II., 101.

III.

POPULATION.

66. Population increases up to the limit of the sustaining power of the land at a given stage of the arts and under a given standard of living, or, mortality and reproduction are equal at the limit, on a given stage of the arts, and with a given standard of living.—Explain and prove this law.

Spencer, Biology, II., 479.   Cairnes, Logical Method, 149-181.
Roscher, II., 273-336.   Mill, I., ch. 10.
Fawcett, Pauperism, Chap. III.

67. What is over-population? What is under-population? British India has 200 to the square mile; Belgium, 469; Rhode Island, 254. Which comes nearer to over-population and which to under-population?

Roscher, II., 337-341.

68. How is the ratio Land : Population affected by advance in the arts and higher standard of living?

Adam Smith, I., 262.

69. The law of population and the law of the diminishing return show that, other things being constant, the human race, in the process of time, must advance towards misery, pestilence, famine and war. State in detail what "the other things" are? Are they constant? If they vary, what makes them do so? Define civilization from this point of view. Show what produces civilization; what it consists of; what its effects are. Do any of your facts or deductions bring out "exceptions" to the laws of population and the diminishing return, or prove those laws untrue?

Princeton Review, November, 1881, p. 303.

70. What is the importance for land rent, wages, rate of interest, and so for the status of the population, of the ratio Land : Population? What is the limit of that ratio?

71. Make a complete catalogue of food-plants and discuss their comparative economic value.

IV.

LAND AND RENT.

72. Discuss the following definitions of rent:

"Rent is that portion of the produce of the earth which is paid to the landlord for the use of the original and indestructible powers of the soil."

Rent is the price paid for the use of an appropriated natural monopoly.

Ricardo, 34.   Walker, 203.   McCulloch's Adam Smith, 444. Adam Smith, I., 151, Rogers's note.

73. State the law of the diminishing return. Mention as many things as you can to which it applies. Why do we find our population scattered sparsely over our whole territory and not concentrated on the Atlantic coast? Why is American agriculture slovenly? Why have our agricultural colleges obtained few students of the science of agriculture? Why is forestry neglected in the United States? Why are we not a pains taking people? Why are we not frugal?

Marshall, 21-26.   Walker, Land, 45-6.

74. If the land of a certain district constituting an economic unit (i. e. such that, with existing means of transportation, no staples of food could profitably be brought into it) were all of a uniform quality, would none of it bear rent?
Adam Smith, I., 151–169, with Rogers's notes.

75. A court has been established in Ireland to adjust rents between landlord and tenant. Is this the same thing as fixing wages or prices by some public authority?
Cairnes, Essays, 202–231.

76. It is argued that the system of "judicial rents" will produce two sets of landlords instead of one. What is the argument? Is it sound? It is argued that fifteen years hence another equally arbitrary interference with contract will be necessary. What is the ground of that argument?

77. Can a class of peasant proprietors be brought into existence by any legislative machinery?

78. What are the social and economic objections to the French system for the inheritance of land? What are the objections to the English custom of settlements?

Mill, V., 10, §4.   Edinburgh Review, XL., 350.
Nation, XV., 218 ; XX., 312.   Le Play, I., 271-293.
Probyn, 122-126 ; 184-212, cf. 108 ; 291-312.
Brodrick, 129-151.   Walker, Land, 212 fg.   Letourneau, 440.
Pollock, 181-5.   Fawcett, Pauperism, chap. VI.

79. Discuss historically and logically this thesis: The tenure of land of the tiller of the soil is always most fixed where personal independence is lowest, and, the more liberty and individualism are developed, the more precarious is the tenure of land.—At what point does fixity of tenure turn from the bondage of the villain to the blessing of the free man?

Cunningham, 54, 97, 111, 197-199.   Seebohm, 176-178.

80. Do you know of any place where the "margin of cultivation" or the "Ricardian acre" can be seen? Where would you look for it? Does it contravene the Ricardian law of rent to show that the "margin of cultivation" for England is in the United States?

81. "Few Irish farms have been able to furnish the family of the actual cultivator with a comfortable subsistence, and leave something over to be contributed to the support of another family in a certain ease. In England, owing to a

greater abundance of capital, and the existence
of manufactures, the landlord has been compelled
to put up with a smaller share, because the farmer's standard of living was higher, and his tra-
ditions of comfort and respectability so strong,
that no landlord could compel him to lower them
in order to pay a greater rent."

82. Definition of a fair rent: "A rent which
might be fairly paid, and yet permit a tenant not
deficient in those qualities of industry and providence which are expected in any walk of life to
live and thrive."

83. Is there any rent on a fishery, or a quarry?
Is there any rent on a water power? Is stump-
age a kind of rent? Is there any rent on a mine?
Note Rogers's comment (Adam Smith, I., 177),
and test his doctrine by the facts of the coal
trade in the United States.
Adam Smith, I., 171–185.   Mill, III., 5, §3.

84. If one man owned New York harbor
could he obtain rent for it? How great would
the rent be? What now becomes of what he
would get?

85. "How are pasture rents, shooting rents, and ground rents of dwellings determined respectively?" (M. 643.)

86. A picture by a great artist and an acre ot land sold in 1825 for the same price. In 1875 the same picture and the same acre changed hands again for ten times as much each. Is there any reason why the state should sequestrate all the increased value ("unearned increment") in one case and not in the other? (M. 725.)

87. It is said that a publisher pays Mr. Tennyson £4,000 per annum for the exclusive right to publish everything written by Mr. T. Is there here anything analogous to rent? If any analogy, how far imperfect?

88. A manager pays a prima donna so much for each evening's performance. How far is there here any analogy to rent?

89. What are *latifundia?* Where can we see *latifundia* to-day, or the nearest resemblance to them?

Letourneau, 424.

90. Discuss the proposition that the United States shall sell no more land without reserving the right to demand in future years the unearned increment. Hitherto the popular land policy in the United States has been that the land should be given away freely, or at a nominal price, to actual settlers. Has this been a mistake? What is the fact about the tenure of land in the theory of American law as compared with the same in the theory of English law?

Sumner, Jackson, 184-191.

91. Under what head would you classify the income of a patentee or an author; wages, profits, or rent? (M. 23.)

92. Write an essay on Village Communities.

Maine. Village Communities; De Lavelaye, Primitive Property; Seebohm, the English Village Community; Wallace, Russia.

V.

WAGES.

93. Mention as many different ways as you know of, in which labor has received, or does receive, remuneration for its share in production.

94. Obviously it is necessary, in order to understand the operation of the industrial system, to trace the steps of one action and reaction with care and detail. But production, exchange, distribution, and consumption, production, exchange, etc., follow each other in a never ending series. They in fact overlap at consumption and production, as when the laborer, his energies revived by sleep and breakfast, takes up his spade and again tills the ground. It is in distribution, however, that the replacement of the capital takes place, and we must begin to study a complete reaction either with consumption or production. It really is immaterial, save that our point of cessation must correspond with our point of beginning. If we follow through one reaction, we shall find that it will cover the consumption, transmutation, and replacement of the capital and a distribution

and adjustment of it to begin a new enterprise.—
Criticise.

95. Wages are the remuneration of labor.

Wages are the sum paid per unit of time by
the employer to the employee, in return for which
the employee contracts to employ his productive
energy during a specified time in such manner as
the employer may direct.

Criticise these definitions.

Cf. Adam Smith, I., 67, 69.

96. Describe in detail the contract or competitive wages system as a part of the modern
industrial system, and show what the relations of
employer and employee and their mutual rights
and duties are in it.   Who constitute the wages
class?   Is there any distinctly differentiated wages
class in the United States?   Under what circumstances is such a class distinctly differentiated?

Walker, Pol. Econ., 379.
Stirling in Grant's Recess Studies, 309–333.
Jenkin, ibid., 171–187.

97. Cairnes argues that we cannot apply the
law of supply and demand to labor, because the
supply of labor is produced by biological forces
and not as commodities are produced.—What is
the fallacy of this argument?

Cairnes, Principles, 152–3.

98. If a change takes place in the supply of labor, will a *proportionate* change take place in wages? (Cf. question 33.)

Rogers, Prices, I., 265, 275.

99. An author who defines wages as the share of labor in the product, writes: "The *industrial* conditions were more favorable to the payment of wages in the United States, while in England the *financial* conditions were more favorable." Does he violate his definition? What is the force of the antithesis in the italicized words?

100. Mill (II., 3, §1 and again p. 207, end of chap. X.) speaks of the laborers as one of the classes amongst whom the *product* is divided. At the beginning of chap. XI. and afterwards, he says that wages are paid out of *capital*. Is there an inconsistency here? If so, what is the cause of it, and how is it to be solved? Does he use two different definitions of " wages "?

Cf. also IV., chap. 3.

Princeton Review, November, 1882, p. 251.

101. Sidgwick (p. 318), commenting on the confusion between product and capital noticed in the last question, says: " This confusion seems to be best avoided by considering the assistance to production rendered by labor—whatever form it may take—as constituting the real capital of the employer who purchases it; and the commodities that continually pass into the consumption of the laborers as their share of the produce."—Criticise this proposition. Note that "assistance" is said to be capital, and the assistance of the employee to be the capital of the employer.

102. Sidgwick says again (same page): "The employer purchases the result of a week's labor, which thereby becomes a part of his capital; and may be conceived, if we omit for simplicity's sake the medium of exchange, to give the laborer in return some of the finished product of his industry."—Criticise this view.

103. "As the employer generally makes a profit, the payment of wages is, so far as he is concerned, but the return to the laborer of a portion of the capital he has received from the labor: so far as the employee is concerned, it is, but the receipt of a portion of the capital his labor has previously produced." How does this doctrine differ from that in the last question?

104. It is held that the laborer is the residual claimant of the product of industry after rent, profits, and wages of superintendence have been paid out of it. — Criticise this doctrine. How, under this doctrine or that of the last three questions, would you account for the great advance in wages and other remuneration of labor after the great Plague of 1348?

Walker, Pol. Econ., 265.   Adam Smith, I., 109, Rogers's note.
Cunningham, 188-195.   Rogers, Prices, I., 265.
Rogers, Work and Wages, chap. VIII.

105. Sidgwick says (p. 322): "What remains after subtracting the aggregate price paid for the use of capital (including land) is obviously the share of labor in the aggregate."—Criticise that doctrine. How would this and the doctrine of the last question differ from the old doctrine that wages and profits are the leavings of each other?

106. Competitive or contract wages and profits are in no sense the leavings of each other. They are not parts of the same whole. The wages come out of capital. Hence one who has no capital of his own, or borrowed, can not become an employer, however great a chance of profit he may see. The profits come out of the product. The two (capital and product) stand, one before and the other after the transmutation of capital which occurs in every period of production, and they are as distinct as the plowman's dinner in April and the farmer's sheaf in August, or as the tailor's coat which he is wearing and the employer's coat which the tailor is making. The complementary parts of capital are raw material and fixed capital. The wages enter into the product, not as an explicit, but an implicit, arithmetical factor. The product consists of the replacement of the capital, profits, and rent. The replacement of the capital consists of wages, raw material, and wear of fixed capital. Hence we get two equations, letting $x =$ wages and $t =$ profits: $x+y+z =$ capital; $(x+y+\frac{z}{m})+t+u =$ product. Capital and product bear no known relation to each other. Hence no ratio of x to t can possibly be derived, although it is plain that an increase of x, other factors remaining constant, would be unfavorable to t.—Expand and criticise.

Mill, I., 2, §2 ; 4, §§1, 2. Cairnes, Principles, 159–180. Walker, Pol. Econ., 380.

107. Wages do not belong in distribution at all. They belong under the head of consumption —productive consumption of capital carried forward and constantly re-applied, from one period of production to another, to sustain society and increase the power of man over nature. Hence the doctrine that wages are paid out of capital is alone consistent with any sound knowledge of the evolution of industry and the growth of society. If we treat economics under two heads, statics and dynamics, discarding the old divisions as unphilosophical, wages will fall in the department of dynamics. They are the tie which unites two parties in the application of capital to production, viz: one who wants to live by the increase of his capital and cannot do so without productive effort; the other, who wants to live by productive effort but cannot do so, in a highly organized society, without capital. Hence the two motives unite them in a contract relation whose general aim is their common interest, but within which their interests are antagonistic. Hence nothing can benefit either which (like limiting production) is hostile to their common interest, and, under free competition, if either of them wins a temporary advantage over the other, he will have to pay it back again with interest, but probably to the net advantage of both. Hence their antagonism, if carried out by legitimate means, is the law of life and growth and not an evil at all. Cf. question 41.—Criticise this doctrine.

108. "The capital of the employer is, by no means, the real source of the wages of even the workmen employed by him. It is only the immediate reservoir through which wages are paid out, until the purchasers of the commodities produced by that labor make good the advance and thereby encourage the undertaker to pur-

chase additional labor."—Show the fallacy. Is
"reservoir" a valid analogy? Suppose that the
product found no purchasers, or was burned up?
Roscher, II., 56.

109. Macleod, whose fundamental proposition
is that "credit is capital," argues that wages
are paid in credit, i. e. that the employer pays
his laborers with bank notes. These notes "have
been part of the 'wages-fund' and have been
'capital' exactly as if they had been sovereigns."
"Hence we see that not only the accumulation
of past profits is brought into the wages-fund,
but also the anticipation of future profits. * *
Every future profit has a present value, and that
present value may be brought into the 'wages-
fund' and made 'capital' of."—Criticise the use
of credit, capital, and money in this argument.
Show that on this argument only, if it should be
admitted, would it be true that wages can come
out of product.
Macleod, II., 120–128.

110. If an industry was generally depressed,
but one employer was, by exception, making
high profits, what rate of wages would he pay?
If an industry was highly prosperous, but one
employer was, by exception, making no profits,
what rate of wages would he pay?
Princeton Review, November, 1882, p. 255.

111. Is it the same thing to say that wages are determined by the supply and demand of labor, and that wages are determined by the ratio of capital available for wages to laborers ready to work?

Mill, II., 11, §1.   Princeton Review, November, 1882, p. 259.

112. What is the effect of an increased demand for commodities on the wages fund?

Cairnes, Principles, 194-200.

113. What is the relation between prices of products and wages of the laborers who make those products?

Mill, II., 11, §2.   Cairnes, Principles, 200–210.
Rogers, Prices, IV., 491.

114. What is the fallacy of connecting wages by a sliding scale with the price of the product?

Marshall, 216.

115. If the intervals at which wages are paid are longer than the period of production in any industry, are the wages paid out of product, or is the employer swindling the employee? If the latter, show how.

116. Cairnes teaches that the capital is divided, at the beginning of the period of production, into

fixed capital, raw material, and wages fund.
Later he argues that, if trades unions could succeed in putting up wages, they would reduce
profits so low as to check accumulation.—Show
the inconsistency and show where the error lies.

Princeton Review, November, 1882, p. 252.

117. What is the effect to be expected on the
wages of laborers from insurance against acci-
dent, sickness, or death, (1) if the employers pay
for it in whole or in part; (2) if " the state" pays
for it in whole or in part?

Fawcett, Pol. Econ., 6th Ed., Chap. XI.

118. It is said that the gains of the venturer
(wages of superintendence) are analogous to rent.
What ground is there for this opinion? Is the
venturer the landlord, the farmer, or the land?

Walker, Pol. Econ., 247–255.　　　Mill, III., 5, §4.

119. If the land of Great Britain should be
confiscated, would the wages of any employments
be affected? If so, which ones, and why?

120. If trades unions should establish a rule
that women should have the same wages as men
wherever they are employed in similar. work,
would that rule be for the benefit of women or of
men?

Mill, II., 14, §5.

121. Suppose that working time should be reduced 20 per cent., what would be the effect on
real wages, on profits, and on prices? Compare
scarcity-high-wages with plenty-high-wages.
Cf. Rogers, Prices, IV., 491.

122. " The maintenance of a standard of comfort among laborers is like the maintenance of a
sea wall; if a section give way all defense is lost.
Examine how far this is true, and investigate the
limits of defensible rules that laborers as a body
may impose on their associates." (M. 409.)
To what extent have trades union rules aimed
at or attained the end of maintaining the standard
of comfort?

123. Do you think that the protective taxes
lower the standard of living of American wage
receivers?

124. Strikes and trades union rules do not
have equal chances of success in all trades.
Their chances are better according as the trade
is a monopoly on account of physical circumstances, or special training, or skill, and according as the public is annoyed by any interruption
of the industry.—Prove this.
Thornton, 340–360.   Marshall, 187–198.   Price, Chap. VIII.
Sumner, What Classes Owe, Chap. VI.

125. Is there any ground for believing that struggles between employers and employees can be done away with by arbitration?   Can arbitration be employed in the making of a contract or is it confined to the interpretation of a contract?
Marshall, 214–217.

126. Is it for the advantage of the wages class to find some new and cheaper article of diet?

Is it for the advantage of the wages class that the wives and children of men of that class should work for wages?

Is it a sign of advance in the community when we see more boys employed as cash boys, messengers, etc.?
Adam Smith, I., 76, 168–170.   Mill, II., 14, §§4, 5.
Walker, Pol. Econ., 321.   McCulloch's Adam Smith, 467.

127. What is the effect on wages of having part of the population soldiers, pensioners, paupers and convicts, or an undue proportion of them priests, monks and civil servants?   Are not such persons withdrawn from competition in the labor supply?   How does your answer bear on the question whether convicts ought to be employed or kept idle?

The farmers of the United States are told that it is for their interest to pay protective taxes to support manufactures, because otherwise the manufacturing population would all compete in agriculture. What is the fallacy of this argument? Connect your answer to this question with the answer to the last?

Sumner, Argument, etc., 7.

128. Discuss briefly the employment of convicts, in its economic aspects; discriminate the cases where they are employed under superintendents, or on a contract system; at the market price or below; all in one trade, or in a number of trades.

Mill, II., 14, §§4, 5.

129. Can the landowners of Great Britain take all the advantage of the natural deposits of coal and metal in that country, and not let British wage receivers have a share in the bounty of nature to their country?

Cairnes, Principles, 54–57.

130. What is the effect on wages and profits of exporting capital?

Can any connection be traced between the exportation of capital and the migration of labor?

Suppose that English capital builds a railroad

in Iowa and an English laborer migrates to Iowa, settles on the railroad line, and cultivates land. What are the economic effects on all the parties interested, and on the wealth of the two countries?

Adam Smith, II., 216, Rogers's note.

131. What is "store-pay?" Show by an analysis of the transaction why it is very injurious to wage receivers. Do the phenomena of store-pay throw any light for the economist on contract wages?

132. An American landowner is often also a mechanic; say, for instance, a carpenter. He builds a barn for some one and agrees to take his pay in a lump sum when the barn is done. What is the economic analysis of such a case? Does it throw any light on the theory of wages?

133. How would the economist describe in the technical language of his science that which the popular dialect describes as "living from hand to mouth?" Describe any persons in savage or civilized life who so live? Can any inferences as to a sound wages system be drawn from the phenomena of living from hand to mouth?

134. "A high rate of wages indicates, not a high, but a low cost of production for all commodities measured in which the wages are high." —Prove this.

Cairnes, Principles, 382–386.

135. "Show how a rise or fall of the average rate of wages within a country acts on its external trade." (M. 435.)

Cairnes, Principles, 318–341.

136. "In the island of Laputa a law was passed compelling each workman to work with his left hand tied behind his back, and the law was justified on the ground that the demand for labor was more than doubled by it. Examine this argument." (M. 443.) Would the human race be better off on earth if each person had only one arm? If a race should be evolved which had four arms, would it be doomed to misery and extinction?

137. Some coal-workers want a diminution of the out-put of coal as a means of keeping up their wages. How far, if at all, would the means accomplish the end? (M. 444.) Would the human race be better off if the richness of the existing deposits of coal was reduced ten per cent.?

138. "The day-laborer, feeling himself more of a man than formerly, must oftener wear a white laundered shirt, but he cannot pay over 50 cents for one. The demand of the higher civilization of the day-laborer must be met, and white laundered shirts are supplied at retail for 50 cents or even for 37 cents. But the wages of the women who make them have been reduced to 8 cents per shirt."—Show the fallacy. Can a man raise his standard of living at the expense of others, just because he wants to? Does true rise in the standard of living of one lower the wages of others?

139. In a shoe town a retail shoe-dealer undersells all his competitors 25 cents per pair. He "obtains from the manufacturer his lowest price for making 100 cases as per sample. He then offers to pay so much—a sum less than the manufacturer's estimate—and pay cash. The manufacturer, rather than lose a good cash order, consents to make the goods, but not being able to reduce the cost of raw materials takes the discount out of labor."—Argued that the wages receivers work against themselves and each other by buying as cheaply as they can. Show the fallacy.

140. Ricardo said (p. 241): "In America and many other countries, where the food of man is easily provided, there is not nearly such great temptation to employ machinery as in England, where food is high, and costs much labor for its production."—Criticise this. What is the fact about the "temptation to employ" labor-saving machinery in the United States, and what is the reason for it?

141. Ricardo goes on: "The same cause that raises [the wages of] labor, [i. e. greater cost at which food is obtained for an increasing population] does not raise the value of machines, and, therefore, with every augmentation of capital, a greater proportion of it is employed on machinery."—Is the doctrine here laid down true? Is the reason given for it correct?

Cairnes, Principles, 174–180.

142. Define and illustrate industrial copartnership. Whence comes the gain by industrial copartnership? Is the principle capable of indefinite extension and application? If not, what are its limits? What permanent good will the plan accomplish, if it is generally employed? Why is it not popular with trades unionists?

Thornton, 363–397.   Fawcett, Pauperism, chap. V.   Taylor.

143. What are the reasons for the gain in coöperative stores? Is the principle of such stores capable of indefinite expansion and application? If not, what is the limit? What would result if coöperative stores should entirely displace private establishments? Will such stores produce a permanent improvement? If so, what will it be?

Thornton, 397-418

144. Coöperation in production and distribution aims to reduce or do away with wages of superintendence. Would this be a great gain? Is it possible?

Holyoake, II., 86.

145. By aiding and encouraging the accumulation of capital, coöperative stores operate a kind of natural selection on the non-capitalist class, selecting out those who have the will and energy to better themselves, and helping them on, while depressing by just so much more those who are shiftless. If the selected women marry only the selected men, the separation between these two sections of what was once one class widens from time to time.—Expand and prove this or refute it.

Holyoake, II., 193-4.

146. Having in mind your answer to the last question, discuss a proposition to provide decent lodgings for the miserable, by the interference of the municipality in a way involving expense to tax payers.

147. Using your answers to the last two questions, show which kind of schemes for social aid favor the survival of the fittest, and which kind favor the survival of the unfittest. Can any scheme have any other effect than one of these two?

148. What is the effect of free common schools on the comparative wages of skilled and unskilled laborers?

What is the effect of free schools, including high schools, on the salary of female teachers?

What is the effect of endowed colleges and seminaries on the salary of clergymen?

What would be the effect of technical and industrial schools, maintained by taxation, on the wages of artisans?

Adam Smith, I., 136-142 ; II., 363, and Rogers's note.

149. "On what does the rate of interest depend? Is it affected by the amount of the currency? Does the rate of interest affect the price of land or stocks?" (M. 561 ; 565.)

* Mill, III., 23, §4.   Jevons, Theory, 277-280.

VI.

CONSUMPTION.

150. The most important phenomenon in distribution, distinguishing distribution from consumption, is the replacement of the capital.—Expand and explain.

151. Show the need of investigating consumption as a department of political economy. Show that the proposition: a demand for commodities is not a demand for labor, is a guiding principle for a correct study of consumption.

152. Translate "A demand for commodities is not a demand for labor" into other and less technical terms in order to bring out its meaning.

153. At the end of a certain period of production A, B, C, D, etc., were each a creditor in the market for $1,000. A bought and took as his share that value in jewelry. B took means of subsistence and lived in idleness while consuming them. C took the same but distributed part amongst

servants who served him while he was idle. D
took the same and gave part to laborers who
dug an ornamental lake in his grounds. E took
the same and gave it to laborers who built a railroad which was not needed and could not pay
working expenses. F took his partly in the
same, partly in tools and seed, and employed
laborers to produce a crop of corn. G took his
in tools, etc., which were wanted by certain
foreigners to whom he lent them on interest.
Thus the second period of production passed.
What was the effect of the course pursued by
each of these men on the capital of the community in the third period of production, and on
the interest of wage receivers in the second
per'od and afterwards?

154. Show that "a demand for commodities is
not, etc.," traverses the following fallacies:

(1) That the spendthrift is the benefactor of
the wage receiver.

(2) That wages paid measure cost of production.

(3) That wages are or may be paid out of
product.

(4) That trades-union rules benefit wage-receivers by "making work."

(5) That we "want work" when we want
wages.

(6) That we need to take measures to "give a circulation to money."

(7) That we want "an industry" when we want goods.

Adam Smith, I., 343-353.   Mill, I., 5, §9.   Marshall, 16.
Cairnes, Principles, 48-54 ; 194-196 ; 249 ; 254.

155. How do the things·which are luxuries vary from time to time? What definiteness can be given to the notion of a luxury?

156. Is there any cause for anxiety on account of the large amount of "foreign luxuries" which are imported into the United States?

157. Luxurious consumption is selfish and unsocial; productive consumption causes activity in a great number and variety of social functions, and multiplies the active relations of the consumer with others.—Criticise this assertion.

158. Discuss the economic effects on a community of an increased expenditure for theatrical and similar entertainments.

159. What judgment is to be passed on "an idle rich man" who has no vices, regarding him and his behavior solely from the economic standpoint?

160. A writer on behalf of the Chinese in California estimates their earnings at fifteen million dollars, and then makes this argument to show the good they do to that State: "Of this sum, ten per cent. having been deducted for savings, thirteen and one-half million dollars will pass into general circulation, remaining to enrich the State, or passing out of it to pay the debts of the general population. It is a stream of wealth which enriches the whole region."—Did he properly use his facts to prove his case?

161. "Luzerne County contains an area of 1,350 square miles. Until the development of the coal trade, the agricultural production of the county was in excess of the home consumption. Now a different state of affairs exists. The rapid increase of population from 1860 to 1870, amounting to 90,000, changed the former order of things, and notwithstanding she contains within her limits some of the most fertile lands in the State, her agricultural productions now fall far short of the amount necessary for home consumption. Nearly one-half of her citizens are non-producers, relying upon the coal interest either directly or indirectly for their employment or support."

162. "If one-third of the present agricultural laborers in the (Western) States would become

mechanics, miners, etc., and thus consumers of
their former products, the other two-thirds
would find no trouble in sending their dimin-
ished surplus to the East at reasonable rates, and
would retain at home the money now sent abroad
to purchase manufactured articles for their own
consumption."

163. State the economic effects to all parties
concerned, on the island and elsewhere, if a certain island, otherwise only sparsely populated,
should become a sanitary resort.

164. An Irish landlord had an income from
rent of £x For four years he kept up a certain
establishment, hiring servants and buying supplies wherever he lived, and exchanging his surplus income entirely for products of France, i. e.
wine, brandy, silks, laces, ribbons, etc. The first
year he lived on his estate, the second in Dublin,
the third in London, and the fourth in Paris.
Was he an "absentee" in his second year? What
was the effect on the wealth of France, England,
or Ireland, or on the interests of any class in any
one of these countries, of his changes in his place
of living?
He then changed his policy. He kept up the
same establishment and hired servants and
bought supplies wherever he lived, as before,

but he saved and made capital of his surplus. The first year he lived in Paris and invested his savings there. The next year he staid in Paris but sent all his savings to Ireland for investment. The third year he lived on his estate in Ireland and invested all his savings there. The fourth year he staid in Ireland, but sent all his savings to Paris for investment. What was the effect of his new policy in each of the four years on the wealth of France and Ireland, and on the interests of any class in either?

165. A owns some land, some railroad stock and a share in a factory, in Colorado. Does the ownership of either of these pieces of property create a duty for him to live in Colorado; if so, of which?

Is there any class in Colorado for whose interest it is that he should live there? If so, what class?

166. Would you say that a man might live anywhere on earth that he chose, undisturbed by the fear lest he was doing wrong, or neglecting his duty to some of his fellow men, by living in one place rather than another? If not, modify the statement as you think necessary.

Would it make any difference with your answer whether you regarded the feudal relations of landlord and tenant as entirely superseded by contract relations, or not?

167. "We are glad to see this determination among millionaires not to be outdone by one another [in building expensive steam yachts]. It is a rivalry in which all take the greatest interest, and by which all are indirectly benefited." "Extravagance, when practiced by millionaires is a blessed thing. It causes a freer circulation of money, affords the laboring man work, feeds women and children, and affects, in fact, every industry, no matter how small."

168. "There was a notion that the money appropriated by the river and harbor bill was thrown away. Where? Probably ninety per cent. went into muscle and labor."

169. Suppose that, by a change in climate, the household consumption of coal in the United States should be reduced one-half, what would be the effect on the wealth of the country? (M. 36.)

170. Suppose that we should succeed in producing a horse-power by electricity at one-half the cost of producing the same by steam, what

would be the immediate and what the ultimate effect on the wealth of the country? and on particular parts of its wealth?

171. Describe the state of society which would be produced if, as fast as capital was accumulated, it was put to productive employment, none of it being consumed luxuriously, and if this was kept up for, say, fifty years.

VII.

MONEY, CURRENCY AND BANKING.

172. Money is any commodity which is set apart by common consent to serve as a medium of exchange. Analyze and justify, or criticise and correct this definition.

173. Is money a measure of value? If so, why not include another specification in the definition? Define carefully "a measure of value." It has been objected that value is a ratio (*e.g.*, ¾) and that we cannot measure a ratio. Is that objection valid? Is money a "denominator of value?" Does "denominator of value" cover all that is correct and essential in "measure of value?"

McCulloch's Adam Smith, 480 fg., and Art. Money in tne Encyc. Britan. 8th ed.

174. Currency is a collective term for all forms of credit instruments by which the use of the medium of exchange (money) is dispensed with, the instruments of credit serving as records and evidence of the rights of the parties until such time as value may be given and received for value. Instruments of credit are not a cheap kind of money. There is no such thing as cheap money. Instruments of credit are not in any sense "substitutes for money," or " representatives of money."—Explain and criticise this definition. Test it in the case of bank-notes, checks, promissory notes, book debts.

175. In barter, one thing is given for another. In the money system, one thing is given for money and money is given for the other. In the credit system, the instruments of credit are not "media of exchange." One thing is given as half of a barter, and a credit instrument (transferable or not) is created as a record and evidence of the fact, and of a debt. When the other thing is given the barter is concluded and the evidence of debt is cancelled. The utility of credit is that it makes money unnecessary.—Criticise and explain. Show why, as credit becomes more general, the function of money as a measure of value becomes more and more important.

176. Show that, historically, money was first invented and used as a measure of value ; that, in time, when the "money system" had superseded barter, the function of money as a medium ot exchange came to predominate ; that the function of measure of value is now again becoming the more important as credit institutions are developed.

177. "Of the money daily used a very small percentage is bank-notes. The great bulk is checks, drafts and telegrams. The telegraph transmits millions upon millions of bank credits from Boston to New York, Chicago, London, etc., etc., and the reverse, where the telegram is the only money used." If, instead of telegraphing, a man should telephone, would his words be money? In the contribution box in church were specie, greenbacks and bank-notes. A gentleman put in his card with $1.00 written in the corner. If the greenbacks and bank-notes were money, was the card money? A play-writer, being under personal obligation to an actor sent him a card on which was written, " Good for a three-act comedy." Was this card money, if greenbacks and bank-notes are money? Is any definition of money possible if it goes beyond the selected commodity ?

178. How would the question, whether Clearing House Certificates are money or not, affect or be affected by different definitions of money ?

179. A public-house keeper gave a glass of beer to a shoemaker and put a chalk-mark on the door against the shoemaker's name. After a certain time the shoemaker made and delivered to the landlord a pair of shoes, thereby cancelling the score. Was the chalk-mark money?, Was it currency? Suppose that the shoemaker had sold the shoes for a bank-note and paid his score with the note, would the note be money? Would it be currency? Would the chalk-mark then be money? Or currency? Suppose that the landlord gave a receipt for the payment, would that be money? Would it be currency? What criticism do these questions suggest on the definition that money is any medium of exchange?

180. Show the fallacy of any definition of money which puts checks in one category and bank-notes in another. Is it a correct criterion to say that bank-notes are taken in "final" payment, or "without recourse?"

Walker, Money, 399.

181. "Credit, no doubt, is a comparatively fragile and perishable instrument for transferring wealth." The "credit" of a banker who is barely solvent, if solvent at all, is said to be part of the capital of the bank, "provided we are careful to point out that such capital is of fragile nature, liable to sudden destruction in case of a panic."—Criticise the notions of credit, capital and medium of exchange. Note especially "fragile."

Sidgwick, 129, 239.

182. Define depreciation and appreciation of the currency. What causes may produce either? What are the effects of either?

More generally, what determines the value of the currency?

Hertzka, 20–76 ; 192–224.   Chevalier on Gold, 124–137.
Cairnes, Essays, 53–77.

183. Define carefully the effect of habit in regard to money.

184. State the law of the distribution of the precious metals.

Walker, Money, Chap. III.

185. A coin is a piece of metal convenient for circulation which is assayed for quality, weighed for quantity, and stamped by authority as a guarantee of weight and fineness.—Expand and explain. Is a coin a highly developed tool? Sketch the history of coins.

Art. Coinage, in Lalor's Cyclopedia.

186. Some say that gold and silver are plainly indicated by Providence as the materials for money; others say that we use gold for money only because it is the most convenient thing we know of for the purpose. Which do you think right?

187. If we work a gold mine, gold comes out. What goes in? On what does it depend whether the community gains or loses by the exchange?
Adam Smith, I., 184; II., 141-4.
Cairnes, Essays, 43-52.

188. What facts go to determine the amount of money which a country needs?
Mill, III., 9, §3.   Roscher I., 366-374.   Chevalier III., 615-650.
Walker, Money, 44-76.

189. May an English cobbler get gold at less cost than a California miner?
Mill, III., 19, §§1, 2.   Cairnes, Essays, 103.
Roscher, I., 378-380.

190. In what respect is it an advantage to get gold first after it leaves the mines? What was the effect on Spain of being the first through whose hands the gold of America passed in the sixteenth century?
Adam Smith, I., 199; II., 86-88.   Cairnes, Essays, 93-108,
Cairnes, Principles, 412-14.

191. One nation having conquered another in war forced it to pay a great war indemnity. Trace the effects on capital, money, prices, wages, profits and credit in each country.

Price, 380–382.

192. France paid to Germany over a thousand million dollars. What were the actual transactions by which this payment was made? Analyze those transactions and show their significance in an economic or financial point of view.

Say, 195.   Giffen, Chap. I.

193. The mint price of gold, .900 fine, at the San Francisco and Philadelphia mints is $18.604. Why then is gold ever shipped from California to New York? (M. 990.)

194. Give the history of the trade dollar? What was the object aimed at by the coin when first coined? Was it a desirable object, and was coining the trade dollar a good means of accomplishing it? What is now the difficulty and danger connected with the trade dollar? What legal ground of obligation exists, if any, why the United States should redeem those coins at par in gold?

195. We read in the money article, " The price for silver bullion in London is 50$\frac{11}{16}$ pence per ounce. Here the bullion value of the 412½ grains silver dollar is $0.849." What is the margin for expenses and profits in exporting a silver dollar to London, exchange being 4.84?

196. What is demonetization?

197. State the causes of the recent change in the relative value of gold and silver.
See authorities under question 202. Crump, 254–267.

198. What have been the great changes in the relative value of gold and silver during the Christian era?
Soetbeer, 114, fg. Chevalier, *Economie Politique*, III., 354–465.

199. Has the ratio 1:15½ for the value of gold to that of silver any historical or scientific prestige over any other ratio? Note that at the end of the 16th century writers on money regarded the relation 1:12 as " normal" or as " given by God and observed by nature."
Soetbeer, 127.

200. The Alternate (or Alternative) or Double Standard consists in a free mint for either gold or silver, the gold and silver dollar (or other unit) having a ratio of weight (fineness being the same) which is fixed by law.

Bimetalism is a project for forming a league of civilized States to carry out an agreement to coin gold and silver at a ratio of 15½ to 1, on the assumption that fluctuations in the value of the metals can in that way be restrained within such limits that there will be a concurrent circulation of the two metals, and that the whole amount of both metals may be available for money.

Expand and explain these definitions. Note especially "free mint" and the function ascribed to law, in the first; also, "project," "league," "15½ : 1," "assumption," "such limits," and the notion about the desirableness of a large supply of money, in the second.

201. Give the history of the French coinage system from 1785 to 1873. Give the history of the Latin Union. Did France resume specie payments in 1878 on the double standard?

Give the history of English coinage since 1700. What brought about the legislation of 1816?

Give the history of coinage in the United States since 1790. What were the motives of the Bland Silver Act? What have been its effects?

Have they been such as the advocates of the act expected? What further effects are to be expected?

Articles on Coinage in Macleod's Dictionary of Political Economy and Lalor's Cyclopedia.

Princeton Review, Nov., 1879, p. 551. Le Touzé, 121-140.

202. The Alternate Standard and Bimetalism or Concurrent Circulation stand on a totally different plane. The former contains no scientific absurdity. The question of adopting it is purely one of expediency. A concurrent circulation is a scientific absurdity and a practical impossibility. It is scientifically as absurd as perpetual motion, or perpetual inertia, because it proposes to annul economic force. It is practically impossible because the league of States would become weaker, not stronger, the more members it embraced.—Expand and prove.

Princeton Review, Nov., 1879. Hertzka, 270-288.

Walker, Pol. Econ., 406-417 ; Money, 243-271 ; Money and Trade, 136-196. Horton, 29-36. Seyd., 584-680. Giffen, 197-207 ; 286-310. Sidgwick, 453-4. Le Touzé, 148-9.

203. "Imagine two reservoirs of water, each subject to independent variations of supply and demand. In the absence of any connecting pipe the level of the water in each reservoir will be subject to its own fluctuations only. But if we open a connection, the water in both will assume

a certain mean level, and the effects of any excessive supply or demand will be distributed over
the whole area of both reservoirs." Show the
fallacy of this analogy to prove that a compensatory action can be established by the mint law
fixing a ratio of value of gold to silver, by which
compensatory action fluctuations in the value of
the metals will be neutralized.

Jevons, Money, 139–40.

204. Supposing that the bimetalic project could
be set going, and that the theory on which it is
based were sound, and that a new supply of gold
should be won from a new California, what would
be the effect on the interests of different parties?

Hertzka, 277.

205. Why did the Latin Union close its mints
against silver in 1874, and following years? Was
the so-called "compensatory action" of the French
system accomplished at a loss to France or not?

Hertzka, 268.

206. If it should be granted that the alternative standard favors debtors, and that it is right
to favor debtors, would that exhaust the effect of
the alternation? If not, what would be its wider
effects on classes and nations?

Hertzka, 291–298.

207. Under the alternate standard the standard of value would have more numerous fluctuations, but less wide fluctuations, than under a single standard.—Prove this. Which is the more important fact in regard to fluctuations, magnitude or frequency?

208. Is anyone the richer by obtaining money unless by way of gift, theft, or gambling? (M. 899.)

209. In 1880 the nickel in a five-cent piece was worth three cents. The silver in four quarters or ten dimes was worth eighty cents—"cents" being hundredths of a gold dollar. A, B, and C each paid a five cent fare. A, paid with a nickel five-cent piece. B, gave a trade dollar which was taken for ninety cents. He received three quarters and a dime in return. C, gave a gold dollar and received three quarters and two dimes. What value in gold did each pay for his ride?

210. Herbert Spencer argued that the function of coining money would have been better performed by private enterprise. Jevons objected that the gain in coining comes from making bad money not good, so that competition would run downwards not upwards. Hence, he thought that coining was a peculiar industry which the State ought to, or must, undertake. A third person, commenting on this difference of Spencer and Jevons, said that, if governments had left coining to individual enterprise, the Rothschilds would have given us a universal money fifty years ago.—Who was in the right, and why?

Jevons, Money, 64, 82. Spencer, Social Statics, 438. Cf. Sidgwick, 450–452.

211. Credit is not a thing but a personal relation. Hence it cannot be capital. It transfers capital.—Expand and illustrate this statement, or refute it, if you think it incorrect. Show the advantages of credit and how it aids industry.

212. A bank is an institution which facilitates the borrowing and lending of capital.—Expand and explain this definition. Show what false notions of a bank it excludes. Does a bank deal in credit or debt? Is it an essential function of a "bank" to issue notes?

Sumner, Jackson, 230, 233–4, 319, 362.

213. BALANCE SHEET OF AN ENGLISH COUNTRY BANK.

Liabilities.	£ million.	Assets.	£ million.
Deposits, ...	1.74	Cash, in London, and at call,	.27
Circulation, . . .	.05	Government funds, . .	.33
Acceptances of London		Indian and colon. gov. secur.,	.44
bankers, . . .	.01	Other securities, . .	.06
Capital, . . .	.18	Discounts, . .	.14
Guarantee fund, . .	.04	Loans, ...	.74
Profit to date, . .	.01	Bank premises, . .	.03
	2.05		2.05

What does this statement show in regard to the kind and proportion of the operations of this bank, its prosperity, and its ability to withstand a financial storm?

Gilbart, 98–108 ; 470–488.

214. BALANCE SHEET OF A SCOTCH BANK.

Liabilities.	£ million.	Assets.	£ million.
Deposits, . . .	10.08	Cash on hand or in London,	2.08
Circulation, . .	.60	Consols and colon. secur.,	1.43
Fourteen day drafts, .	.13	Bk. of Eng. and other stocks,	.38
Acceptances, . .	.17	Discounts, . . .	6.85
Capital, ...	1.00	Short loans, . .	1.58
Rest or reserve, . .	.75	Secur. against acceptances,	.17
Semi-ann. dividend, .	.07	Bank premises, . .	.20
Balance, . . .	.02	Property paying rent, .	.13
	12.85		12.85

What can you learn from this statement about the kind of business which the bank is carrying on, its prosperity, and its power to stand against a financial storm?

Gilbart, 489–522. Macleod, Dictionary, Banking in Scotland.

215. BALANCE SHEET OF A LONDON JOINT STOCK BANK.

Liabilities.	£ million.	Assets.	£ million.
Deposits, . . .	23.09	Cash and in Bk. of Eng., .	2.86
Circular notes etc., .	.56	Money at call and short	
Acceptances, . . .	.52	notice, . . .	3.71
Endorsements, . .	.07	Government securities, .	3.57
Capital, ...	2.80	Indian gov. secur., .	.75
Rest, ...	1.64	Discounts and loans, .	17.15
Profits, ...	.25	Liability of customers for	
		acceptances, . .	.52
		Liability of customers for	
		endorsements, . .	.07
		Bank premises, . .	.30
	28.95		28.95

Criticise as in question 214.

Gilbart, 462–470.   Crump, 23–32.
Bagehot, 243–266.

216. WEEKLY STATEMENT OF THE BANK OF ENGLAND.

ISSUE DEPARTMENT.

	£ million.		£ million.
Notes issued, . . .	38.01	Government debt, . .	11.01
		Other securities, .	4.73
		Gold coin and bullion, .	22.26
	38.01		38.01

BANKING DEPARTMENT.

	£ million.		£ million.
Proprietors' capital, .	14.55	Government securities, .	13.67
Rest, ...	3.09	Other securities, .	20.13
Public deposits, . .	3.51	Notes, ...	11.90
Other deposits, . .	25.02	Gold and silver coin, .	.68
Seven day and other bills,	.22		
	46.40		46.40

The Old Form.

Liabilities.	£ million.	Assets.	£ million.
Circulation, . . .	26.33	Securities, . . .	35.01
Public deposits, . .	3.51	Coin and bullion, .	22.95
Private deposits, . .	25.02		
	54.87		57.96

Balance £ 3.09 mill. as in the Rest above.
Rate of discount, 3 per cent.

Describe from this statement the organization and operation of the bank. How much was the " reserve?" What was the per centage of reserve to cash liabilities? Give the same points as in the last three questions.

Gilbart, 21–71 ; 254–277.   Crump, 268–307.   Price, 419–436.
Bagehot, 160–243.   Hankey, 73–124.

217. What are the peculiarities in the condition of the bank in each of the following statements?

ISSUE DEPARTMENT.

	£ mill.		£ mill.
Notes issued, . . .	49.2	Gov. debt, . . .	11.0
		Other secur., . .	3.9
		Gold coin and bullion, .	34.2
			49.2

BANKING DEPARTMENT.

	£ mill.		£ mill.
Capital, ...	14.5	Government securities, .	15.2
Rest, ...	3.6	Other securities, . .	16.0
Public deposits, . .	6.5	Notes, ...	21.4
Other deposits, . .	28.2	Coin, ...	.8
Seven day and other bills,	.3		
	53.4		53.4

Discount, 2 per cent.

What was the active circulation?

ISSUE DEPARTMENT.

	£ mill.		£ mill.
Notes, ...	33.7	Gov. debt, . . .	11.0
		Other secur., . .	3.9
		Gold coin and bullion, .	18.7
			33.7

BANKING DEPARTMENT.

	£ mill.		£ mill.
Capital.	14.5	Gov. secur., . . .	11.7
Rest, . . .	3.1	Other secur., . .	20.7
Public deposits, . .	3.9	Notes, ...	7.4
Other deposits, . .	18.4	Coin, ...	.6
Seven day and other bills,	.4		
	40.5		40.5

Discount, 9 per cent.

ISSUE DEPARTMENT.

	£ mill.		£ mill.
Notes, ...	21.1	Gov. debt, . . .	11.0
		Other secur., . .	3.0
		Gold coin and bullion, .	6.6
			21.1

BANKING DEPARTMENT.

	£ mill.		£ mill.
Capital, ...	14.5	Gov. secur., . . .	9.4
Rest, ...	3.5	Other securities, . .	26.1
Public deposits, . .	5.3	Notes, ...	.9
Other deposits, . .	12.9	Coin, ...	.5
Seven day and other bills,	.8		
	37.0		37.0

Discount, 10 per cent.

218. STATEMENT OF A NATIONAL BANK.

Liabilities.	$ thousand.	Resources.	$ thousand.
Capital, ...	464.	Loans and discounts, .	708.
Surplus, . . .	203.	Over-drafts, . .	.1
Undivided profits, . .	53.	Bonds to secure circula-	
Circulation, .	404.	tion (par value), . .	450.
Deposits, . . .	419.	Other stocks and bonds,	163.
Due banks, . .	27.	Due from reserve agents,	105.
		" " banks, . .	21.
		Banking house, .	32.
		Current expenses and taxes,	3.
		Checks and cash items, .	4.
		Exchanges for Clear. House.	11.
		Notes of other banks, .	15.
		Gold, . . .	30.
		Silver, ...	.9
		Legal tenders, . .	9.
		Redemption fund in U.S.T.,	20.
	$1,574.		$1,574.

Criticise this statement in the same manner as in question 214.

H. A. Richardson, National Banks.

219. "So many convertible bank-notes will the public use as it has a positive need for in paying with bank-notes and no more."—Expand and explain. How does this assertion bear on the question whether "paper is better than specie?"

Price, 418.

220. Criticise the notion of what a banker does which appears in the following: "We have to consider that the banker to a great extent produces the money he lends, viz: his own obligations, which so long as his business flourishes, he is practically never compelled to redeem; and that he may easily afford to sell the use of this commodity at a price materially less than the rate of interest on capital generally." A banker's rate for commercial bills may be less than the rate of interest "since a comparatively low rate of interest on the medium of exchange inexpensively produced by the banker himself would be sufficient to give him normal profit on his banking capital." For "banker" read counterfeiter and so test the notion.

Sidgwick, 262.   Price, 444–458.

221. A banker "may be only just able to pay what he owes to others, and yet be, so long as his credit lasts, a wealthy man. Suppose that he owes £1,000,000 (without interest) [deposits. etc.], and has debts of merchants, railway companies and the government, which together could be sold for £1,000,000. If there were a run on the bank and he had to suspend payment, his wealth would be found equivalent to zero; but meanwhile he obtains the interest on £1,-000,000, which will leave him a handsome surplus after paying the expenses of the bank. And since there is no reason why he shall not continue to enjoy this surplus for an indefinite period, his business might obviously be sold for a considerable price, even though its assets did not balance its liabilities, provided that the sale were a secret one, so that its credit could be maintained." Would such a man add to the wealth of the country? We formerly had bankers of this description in the United States but we came to regard them as swindlers. Were we wrong?

Sidgwick, 129.

222. Define the "currency principle" and the "banking principle."

Walker, Money, 422-442; Pol. Ec., 178-180.

223. How would you calculate the value to a national bank of its circulation? Suppose that a bank is formed on 4 per cent. bonds which cost

122 and have 20 years to run, the rate of discount being 5 per cent., what is the profit on the circulation?

224. "Explain the remark of an eminent banker: 'If a customer asked me to lend him 10,000 sovereigns, I should answer: Withdraw. If he asked me to lend him 10,000 pounds, I should answer: Let us discuss the matter.'" (M. 1065.)

225. "What would be the effect if all the bank-notes in the Banking Department of the Bank of England were suddenly destroyed?" (M. 1152.)

226. In a period of depression there is just as much currency in the country as ever, but large sums lie in banks, and the rate of discount on call loans is exceedingly low. Why? (M. 1220.)

227. What is the money market? What is dealt in there? What more correct designations might be used?

228. What is the difference between stocks and bonds? What are preferred stocks and second mortgage bonds? What are coupon and registered bonds?

229. It is taught that the rate of interest depends on the supply and demand of capital. In times of crisis excessive rates of interest are paid for the loan of bank notes, even of a suspended bank. Why? and how is such a fact to be reconciled with the doctrine first stated?

Adam Smith, I., 357.   Walker, Money, 94–98.

230. Define carefully legal tender, showing what it is and what it is not. Could Congress make bits of colored paper circulate by declaring them "legal tender?"

Princeton Review, November, 1879, p. 561.

231. Which is the better kind of paper currency, a government issue (greenbacks) or an issue guaranteed by the government (national bank notes)? Give reasons in full.

232. If we had no public debt could we have no national banks? or no national currency? If greenbacks should be called in, paid, and burned, and if the national bank note currency should all be surrendered, and if no state banks were allowed to issue notes, what would be the effect on our interests or our convenience, and what should we probably do?

233. Apply the theory of value to inconvertible paper currency issued by a government.

234. Whenever instruments of credit are generally used as the solvents of contracts, and as the things which are passed from hand to hand instead of money, and in order to avoid the use of money, such instruments of credit bear upon their face the word "dollar," "pound," "franc," etc., by which they refer to coined money which has acquired a traditional and habitual, but variable purchasing power. What is the difference between a bullion note, a convertible bank note, and an inconvertible treasury note, in their relation to the coin whose name they bear?

235. The "fiat money" doctrine is that the government stamp gives the value to a coin; that the "dollar" is an ideal unit; and that the government can just as well issue a note bearing the inscription: "This is one dollar by Act of Congress." What effect would it have on this theory if at the same time a new name should be invented for the "ideal unit of value," say, a "Washington," and the note should read: "This is one Washington by Act of Congress?" Could

such a note "measure value?" If not, how or
why could a greenback do so before 1879?
Walker, Money, 280–290.

236. If the United States should issue "fiat
money" now, how would it be brought into circulation ?
Walker, Money, 288–289.

237. Can you trace any connection or relation
between paper money inflation and the rise of
city real estate?
Mann, Chap. X.

238. "A shrinking volume of money transfers
property unjustly, and causes a concentration
and diminution of wealth. It also impairs the
value of existing property by eliminating from it
that important element of value conferred upon
it by the skill, energy and care of the debtors
from which it is wrested."

239. The people of Guernsey wanted a market, but had not money with which to build it.
The governor issued paper money, receivable
for taxes and dues to the island government, in
sufficient amount to pay for the market. In ten

years the market earned its cost, which was paid into the treasury in the paper money, which was then burned, "and they got a market for nothing— only the credit of the island."

Cf. Jevons, Money, 204.

240. Describe the Clearing House and define the economic advantages of it.

Jevons, Money, 263–289.   Gilbart, Banking, 451–461.

241. Describe the Check Bank.

Jevons, Money, 290–298.
Macleod, Economical Philosophy, II., 510–514.

VIII.

INTERNATIONAL EXCHANGES.

242. "Is there any essential difference between trade between country and country, and trade between county and county, or even between man and man? What is the real nature of trade in all cases?" (M. 1227.)

Cairnes, Principles, 305–6.

243. "We may often, by trading with foreigners, obtain their commodities at a smaller expense of labor and capital than they cost to the foreigners themselves." Explain this.

ι Mill, III., 17, §§2, 3, 4, 5.

244. Define comparative cost of production and show its importance to the doctrine of international trade.

Cairnes, Principles, 307-317.

245. Jevons argues that England never could import coal and carry on her industries in competition with those from whom she bought the coal, the cost of transportation being a constant

premium on the transfer of the industry. Do we not see coal brought from Pennsylvania, Maryland and Virginia to New England to be used in industry? How does that fact bear on Jevons' doctrine? What is the correct inference?

Jevons, Coal Question, Chap. XIII.

246. Jevons argues that coal is exported from England as a return cargo and is essential to her commerce on that account. Why so? Suppose that she should use up her coal and try to import Pennsylvania coal, what obstacle to that would be interposed by the same doctrine when viewed from this side?

247. Give a schedule showing the headings of the accounts which enter into the international exchange. Show from this how fallacious must be any inference about the welfare of the country from the preponderance of imports or exports of merchandize and specie.

248. Suppose that the English wheat crop fails and England imports wheat in great quantities from the United States. How would this probably affect the price of bills of exchange on England, and the price of English products in America?

Mill, III., ch. 20.

249. "He hoped that [the three per cent. loan] would be taken entirely by our own people, so that the country would be saved from the annual drain of a large sum which must otherwise go abroad."

250. The English law ordains that 1869 sovereigns shall be cut from 40 troy pounds of gold, $\frac{11}{12}$ fine. The French law ordains that 3100 francs shall be cut from a kilogram of gold $\frac{9}{10}$ fine. The law of the United States prescribes that the dollar unit shall weigh 25.8 grains of gold, $\frac{9}{10}$ fine. What is par of the metals between the United States and each of the others, and between England and France?

Seyd, 285-290, 301, 346.   Le Touzé, 207-223.

251. What is the difference between long and short exchange?

Seyd, 427-433.

252. How is it that it is a mere matter of usage whether we say that exchange has risen, or that it has fallen, when we mean that it has turned in favor of importers?

253. Give a history of the suspension of specie payments by France, 1871—1878. Show how the

currency was regulated while inconvertible, and what currency doctrines were established by that experience.

Bonnet, two Essays on the Payment of the Indemnity and the Management of the Currency. Translated. Appleton: 1875. *Journal des Economists*, 15th December, 1874 (Wolowski).

254. Is it a benefit or an injury to the United States that a part of the public debt is held in Europe?

255. We read in the money article, "Posted rates of sterling exchange were 4.82 and 4.84½. Rates for actual business were as follows: Sixty days, 4.81 and 4.81½; demand 4.83¾ @ 4.84; cables, 4.83¾ @ 4.85; commercial bills were 4.79½ @ 4.80."—Explain this statement in detail. The minimum rate of discount at the Bank of England was 3 per cent. Perform the arithmetical calculation to show why the sixty day bills and demand bills differed just as they did.

Goschen, Chap. IV.

256. American securities are sold in London at an arbitrary rating, £1=$5.00. Why is this arbitrary rating adopted? News was received that 1000 shares of stock owned in New York had been sold and paid for in London at 120 per share. Cable transfers were 4.85. Brokerage was ⅛ of one per cent. on the par value. What was the net cash value in New York of the return for the stock?

257. In 1832 silver was the standard of the United States, the silver dollar containing 371.25 grains pure silver. The sovereign contained 113.002 grains pure gold. The ratio of value of gold to silver was 15.625 : 1. The traditional par of exchange was \$4.44=£1. What per cent. was the true par of the metals of this assumed par?

258. Show, in a gold-producing country, what the relations and interaction of new gold supply, prices, relative amount of imports and exports, and rate of exchange would be.

259. Let it be assumed that 5,000 Americans go to Europe for the summer, and spend on an average \$1,000.00 each; that if they did not go to Europe they would spend that amount of money in American watering-places. State the economic effects of this European travel on different classes of the population in Europe and America?

260. "Whenever our gold is shipped to Europe, it is noticed that we are spending more than we are earning, and whenever a country with our boundless and diversified resources finds the balance of trade against it, every sensible man and woman should understand that it means retrenchment or ruin."

261. "One of the virtues of extending the hand of welcome to the Chinese is shown by the fact that to-morrow one thousand of these leeches leave San Francisco for Hong Kong bearing $750,000 which they have made in this country. More than 800 of them have, moreover, been provided with return certificates, which enables them to return and take away more of our money."

262. "In earlier days the leather made [in California] was shipped abroad or to the East, and some portion of it was returned in manufactured forms. The consumer had thus to pay in the price of his purchases the cost of two or more expensive shipments, and of several commissions. It cannot be for his interest to do this, nor for the interest of the cattle raiser, who produces hides, for that of the tanner who prepares them, nor in the broadest sense for the interest of the country."

IX.

ECONOMIC POLICY:

Socialism, Adjustment of Rights, etc.

263. What are the characteristics of an industrial civilization? How does the tone and temper of a people trained under an industrial civilization differ from that of a people trained in a military or police state? Show that socialism is at war with industrial civilization.

Spencer, Sociology, I., 584–590 and fg.; II., 603–642.

264. In a modern free state, should the question be: Why let alone? or: Why not let alone?

Sumner, What Classes Owe, Chap. VIII.

265. Prove that state regulation of education, factories, food, lodging, etc., is all illusory so long as the state does not regulate family life, or that, if the state is to regulate at all effectively, it must regulate the family.

Letourneau, 401–2. Rae, 190.

266. Try to make a formula to define the limits of state interference.

Adam Smith, II., 306.   Woolsey, I., 243–269.
Humboldt.   Mill on Liberty.   Baden-Powell, Chap. I
Spencer, Social Statics, Essays.
Rogers, Art. Free Trade, 9th ed. Encyc. Britannica.
Sumner, What Classes Owe, 112–153.

267. If it could be proved to a laborer that a man of his class in the 13th century had better and surer food and clothes than he, he would not for a moment think of returning to the complete status of the 13th century, just on account of what distinguishes the 19th century from the 13th, viz: personal liberty, independence, and civil rights; but these are the blessings of which free competition is the price.—Criticise this assertion.

Cunningham, 387–410.

268. A certain job being offered for competitive bids, one man bid much below any others, being very anxious to get it, and being willing to employ certain means which other contractors disliked, but by which he could make important savings. When the bids were opened his was rejected because, as he was told, he would ruin himself. His plea that he knew his own business was disregarded.—What light did this case throw on competition and *laissez-faire?*

269. The individual's worst troubles come from the cases where the state *cannot* let him alone, because it adopts lines of policy to which he must conform. E. g.: If the state issues paper money no man can separate himself from those who like paper money, and go his own way on his own judgment. The incidental inconveniences of *laissez-faire* are not to be compared with the positive evils endured by a wise minority forced to yield to a foolish majority.— Expand, prove, and collect other instances. Show that the philosophical basis of *laissez-faire* is in the fact that we cannot tell, before the event, who is wise and who foolish.

270. Roscher says: " There is what we might call a public conscience concerning merit and reward, by which a definite relation of the three branches of income to one another is declared equitable. Every ' fair-minded man' feels satisfied when this relation is realized, and this feeling of satisfaction is one of the principal conditions precedent to the prosperity of production, inasmuch as on it depends the participation of all owners of funds and forces." Does this passage describe facts?

Roscher, II., 166.   Walker, Polit. Econ., 281–286.

271. If a man takes an axe and goes into the woods to cut wood, what is a "just" return for his day's labor? Suppose that one man's wood lot is half a mile from home and another's five miles from home, is there any case here under the head of "justice?" Can we say that a man "must" get profits on the capital in the axe and wages for his time? What would be the difference in regard to "just" and "must" if another man owned the wood-lot, provided the axe, and contracted with the first man to go and chop the wood?

272. Each productive laborer puts a share into the combined social productive effort, and each gets some share in the total social satisfaction. The proportion of the effort to the satisfaction is determined by supply and demand, under the existing conditions of the industrial system. There can be no possible conception of a "just" return, or of "justice," in this connection, except the true ratio of effort to satisfaction produced by the free play of supply and demand under existing circumstances. — Criticise this statement. Does "justice" have anything to do with the question whether A and B get as favorable a ratio of satisfaction to effort, one as the other? Suppose that A were an artisan and B a flunkey.

273. Distinguish between the right to get, possess, and enjoy property, and the right to be a property-holder. Which is true and which false? What is the fallacy of any notion of natural rights? Is there any physical or metaphysical good which is gratuitously bestowed on the human race? Show that "equality" never can belong to *being* or *having*, but only to the conditions, chances, and burdens which are created by the state.

De Lavelaye, Preface, and 348–353. Rae, 186.
Sumner, What Classes Owe, 13–15 ; 134–136 ; 163–169.

274. What classes emigrate from Europe to the United States? What classes emigrate from the United States to Europe? Why are the facts as they are?

275. Do you think that there is a tendency of enlightened opinion toward the establishment of a right in every man born on earth to go to, and live on, any part of the earth where he thinks that the environment will be most favorable for such a man as he is? If not, state what modifica_ tion you would want to make in that doctrine of right before you would assent to it.

276. If a man owns some land, a horse, and a plow, is there any difference in the meaning of "property" as applied to each of those things? If so, what is it?

Rae, 446.

277. What are vested rights? What significance have they for the happiness of man and as regards the end for which the state exists? Why do some of the greatest difficulties and dangers of a progressive and liberal state arise from them?

Mill, II., 2, §2.

278. To pull down those who are superior in wealth, culture, talent, virtue, or education is to act like an army invading a hostile country, which should shoot its own advance guard.— Expand and prove this, or correct and refute it.

279. Can any person be held under obligation to contribute to the struggle for existence of any other person, unless the former be shown to be in some way responsible for the latter's existence?—If so, who? and on what grounds?

Mongredien, Wealth, 233.

Sumner, What Classes Owe.

280. Is there any human being who, in any conceivable circumstances, can rightfully say: "I must live"?

281. It is affirmed that the most efficacious cause of the accumulation of great properties is allowing women to inherit on an equal footing with men. Is that true? If so, what bearing does it have on current discussions about inequality of possessions? Would it be, in other respects, desirable to reverse the tendency of modern times in regard to the property rights of women?

Letourneau, 184, 433-4.   De Lavelaye, 217–220.

282. A Connecticut farmer declared that he could not "make any money" because he could not hire any laborers. He said that they all demanded too high wages. A New York merchant declared that he could not "make any money" because his landlord demanded an extravagant rent; the landlord declaring that another tenant was ready to pay the rent demanded. A person who had no capital, but who wanted to carry on business, complained that he could "make no money" because he had to pay such high rates of interest for capital which he borrowed. State the true significance of the facts alleged in each case. What is the correct criticism on these complaints when analyzed and generalized? What should we say of a proposed law to provide one with laborers at wages to suit him, another with a store at rent to suit him, and the third with capital at a rate to suit him?

283. "State what you believe to be the chief economic arguments in favor of the succession of relatives to the property left by deceased persons, instead of its lapse to the state." (M. 238.)

Mill, II., 2, §3.   Letourneau, 440.

284. Distinguish between different kinds of factory acts and state their justification. (M. 1386.)

285. Is there the same justification for industrial schools (teaching trades) as for common schools (giving general culture)? (M. 1390.)

286. Is compulsory school attendance justifiable when tax-payers are forced to provide schools?·

287. "These wretched people (in the slums of London) must live somewhere, and it must be near the center, where their work lies. It is notorious that the Artisans' Dwelling Act has, in some respects, made matters worse for them. Large spaces have been cleared of fever-breeding rookeries to make way for the building of decent habitations; but the rents of these are far beyond the means of the abject poor. They are driven to huddle more closely together in the few loath-

some places still left to them, and so Dives makes a richer harvest out of their misery, buying up property condemned as unfit for habitation, and turning it into a gold mine, because the poor must have shelter somewhere, even though it be the shelter of a living tomb. The State must make short work of this iniquitous traffic and secure to the poor the rights of citizenship, the right to live in something better than fever dens, the right to live as something better than the uncleanest of brute beasts. This must be done before the Christian missionary can have much chance with them."

288. Would it be expedient for a State to expend capital in creating a colony and persuading its emigrating citizens to go to that colony, rather than to let them go whithersoever their interest might lead them? Would it be for the interest of either Germany or the United States that German immigrants should take possession of one State of this Union and make it a " German State?"

Roscher, II., 371.   Adam Smith, II., 134–225.

289. An argument for government favor to capitalists by *not* placing the interest on government bonds at the lowest market rate:

"If we were dealing with the money-lenders of Europe the question would be entirely different; but we are dealing with our own people ; we are dealing with women, with children, with those whose property is in the hands of guardians and trustees; with the farmer who has laid aside temporarily a little money ; with the merchant who has a little balance which he desires to invest in a security which shall be not only absolutely safe but which he may convert at any moment without loss.　Do we want to stand—if I may use the word—jewing with this class of people to see whether this rate of interest shall be 3½ or 3¼ or 3 per cent.?　We must remember that what the government will save by cheapening the rate of interest this class of people of whom I have spoken will to a great extent lose."

290. An American hotel-keeper who failed said that "one of the drawbacks with which hotel-keepers have to contend is the constant increase of rent demanded by our landlords just as soon as they discover we are making a dollar." If the principle of the Irish land act is sound should not the legislature appoint a commission to examine into the truth of the alleged fact, and, if it be found true, should not a court be appointed to assess the "fair rent" of a hotel?

291. On what grounds may railroad land grants be justified?

292. It is objected to patents that they establish property in an idea or device, but that no property in an idea or device should be recognized because two men, or any number of men, can use the same idea or device without interfering with each other, or using it up, but that property in land or chattels is recognized because two men cannot use or enjoy them at the same time. It is also objected that patents are given only for *priority*, not for the invention, and that, within the period of the patent, many persons might independently work out the invention, but are debarred from using it, even for themselves, by the patent law.—Criticise these arguments.

293. "A copyright is a patent under another name and applied to another class of objects, writings instead of inventions."—Is that statement correct? Distinguish thoroughly between copyrights on the one side and patents and tariff monopolies on the other.

Ford, II., 58.

294. Why is transportation a matter of so much greater importance in the United States than in England, France or Germany, and why

are transportation questions so much more diffi-
cult here?

295. It is said that a railroad pool does away
with competition. Why is that not quite correct?

296. What are income bonds? What are col-
lateral trust bonds?

297. The trunk lines, by agreement, charge one
cent per bushel for elevator work at New York,
Baltimore and Philadelphia. The New York
railroad commissioners urged that this charge
should be abolished at New York. The representatives of the railroads replied that to do so
would put the port of New York at a disadvantage. At other ports steamships lie alongside of
the pier on which the elevator is, and there is an
elevator charge of one cent per bushel. In New
York the ships will not come to the elevator but
the grain must be lightered in floating elevators.
The roads pay lighterage, three-fourths of a cent
per bushel, and charge elevator charge of one
cent. If the elevator charge were abolished at
one place, it would be at all, and that would
leave New York at a disadvantage.

Criticise this allegation and inference.

Report, Hepburn Committee, 22–25, 33–4.

298. What is watering stocks? Specify as many varieties of it as you can think of. Could a house, a newspaper, or a race-horse, be "watered" in the same way? Why do we never hear of it? Why should anyone desire to water stocks?

299. A subscribed three shares in a company at par. He received twelve per cent. dividend and the stock was quoted at 200. The company increased its capital in order to extend its business. It did so by allowing each owner of three shares to subscribe for and get one new share for $100. A sold his "right" for $75. After the increase the stock was quoted at 175. Analyze this operation and show its significance for the rights and interests of the public or of any parties concerned.

300. How would you capitalize a newspaper, a lease, a patent right? A company is formed to build a railroad. They subscribe for first mortgage six per cent. bonds in sufficient amount to build it. When it is done they make a stock capital for it. Why do they adopt this method? Criticise it. What should be or may be the amount of the stock capital? This stock capital is said to be "all water." What is meant by

that and is it true? What, if any, property or valuable thing is behind that stock? What is meant by "capitalizing the road at all which the traffic will bear?" It is said' to be a wrong to the public to do that. Why? What do you think about it?

301. It is argued against watering stocks that if a railroad doubles its stock it has to raise its rates for freight and passengers so as to force the public to pay profits on the increased stock.— Criticise that argument, taking note of the two cases, one where the road is a monopoly and the other where it is in full competition with others.

302. A few able and unscrupulous men combined and bought, at a low rate, the stock of a railroad which was well situated but badly managed. They subscribed new capital, put it in good order, paid a dividend, and issued a glowing report. The stock rose to a high figure. They then doubled the stock and also issued bonds on the road for a large amount. They paid large dividends on the watered stock and the half shares were soon as high as the whole ones were before. They then bought up parallel and branch roads at low rates and sold them to the former railroad for its bonds. These and

their stock they then sold. Next they ceased to pay dividends and issued a gloomy report. Thereupon the stock fell and they bought it again.—What had " watering stocks " to do with these transactions? What had issuing annual reports to do with them?

303. A patentee found after a few years that his patent brought him in $5,000 a year. Nine capitalists subscribed $5,000 each to buy of him nine-tenths of his right. The ten then subscribed $5,000 each and formed a joint stock company to develop the patent. It had still ten years to run and they expected that it would earn at least an average of $25,000 per year for those ten years. They put the capital of the company at x dollars, of which each of the ten took one-tenth at the start. What difference did it make to any body what the value of x was? If you were one of the ten, at what value would you want x put, and for what reasons?

304. Write a short essay on the postal telegraph. Consider the possibility that telegrams might be sent at a uniform rate as letters now are.

Jevons, Social Reform.

305. Write a short essay on the purchase of all railroads by the federal government.

306. Write a short essay on the nationalization of the land.

Fawcett, Pol. Econ., 6th ed., Chap. XI.　　DeLavelaye, 320–1.

307. Write an essay on "National Education," i. e., on the proposition, in various forms, to have the federal government meddle with education.

X.

ECONOMIC POLICY :

Public Finance.

308. In what circumstances is it possible to reduce the interest on the public debt?
Leroy-Beaulieu, II., 365–376.

309. Is it possible to pay off a public debt too rapidly? What is the effect of paying it very rapidly?
Sumner, Jackson, 266–72.

310. What measures the burden to a people of their debt?

Is it right to put the extraordinary expenses of this generation as. a burden on the next? On what grounds might an argument be made for so doing?

If a nation is young and growing, what will be the fact with regard to the burden of the debt from decade to decade. How does this fact bear upon the policy of heavy taxation now to pay the debt of the U. S. speedily?
Leroy-Beaulieu, II., 308–311 ; 360–363.

311. What was the experience of England with a "sinking fund" between 1790 and 1828?
Hamilton, 80–171.   Leroy-Beaulieu, II., 306–322.
Accounts and Papers, 710.

312. Has the United States ever had similar experience?
Seybert, 759–774.

313. What is the arrangement about the sinking fund of the federal treasury now? Is the sinking fund of any use or necessity aside from the contract with the bond-holders? Has it any value in fact for them?
W. A. Richardson, 82–85.

314. Show that a sinking fund is not a force in itself, and never can do anything towards the payment of a debt beyond just the amount of saving which is put into it.

315. What was the fallacy of deductions from compound interest which were made the basis of sinking fund doctrines a century ago?

316. How is the reduction of the English debt now accomplished instead of using a sinking fund?
Accounts, etc., 720.

317. What are exchequer bills? What is the theory of their use?

Bagehot, chap. IV.

318. It is argued by very sound and conservative economists on the continent of Europe that it is expedient to connect a drawing of prizes with drawings of the public debt for payment, because fortune and misfortune enter into human life, and constantly affect the managers of capital, so that to offer the small fund holder a chance of a bit of good fortune is only to give him a chance of the same kind.—Criticise this argument.

Leroy-Beaulieu, II., 246-250.

XI.

ECONOMIC POLICY:

Taxation.

319. Define taxation. Show its relations to economic science and statecraft. Show what importance it has for the welfare of the people. Distinguish between arbitrary exactions by irresponsible officials where public peace and security are not assured; taxes laid for other purposes than revenue and having no relation to good government; and strictly economical taxation for which the citizen gets peace, order, and security.

320. The discussion of the canon that taxation should be equal has been much confused by the fact that the disputants sometimes mean equal with respect to units of commodity or property or income, and sometimes equal with respect to the personal circumstances of the different individuals taxed.—Expand and explain this statement.

321. Taxes diffuse themselves on the line of least resistance.—Expand and prove.

322. The parties to an exchange share in all the burdens and hindrances of the same in the direct ratio of their eagerness for the exchange, and they share in the profits and advantages of the same in the inverse ratio of their eagerness for the exchange. This applies to taxes, freights, etc.—Prove this proposition.

Mill, III., 8, §2.

323. From what sources are the revenues of Great Britain obtained now? From what sources are the revenues of the United States obtained? Make a comparison of the two systems of revenue.

Wilson, 109–130. Ford, II., 137–149.

324. Give the history of financial reform in England during the second quarter of this century.

Wilson, 66–85. Mongredien, Free Trade.
Martineau, vols. 2, 3 and 4.
Levi, British Commerce.

325. What are the main points in the Peel-Gladstone system of national finance?

Giffen, Chap. IX.
Molesworth, England, II., 50–228 ; II., 380,—III., 225.

326. "Under what circumstances are taxes on wages transferred to the employer of labor?" (M. 1555.)

Adam Smith, II., 460–463 ; 466–472.   Mill, V., 3, §4.

327. Criticise the Prussian class-tax.

Leroy–Beaulieu, I., 276–280; II., 459–461.

328. Discuss the arguments for and against a legacy and succession tax.

Adam Smith, II., 453–4.   Mill, V., 2, §7.   Jevons, Coal, 365.
Leroy–Beaulieu, I., 489–500.   Letourneau, 440.
Sumner, What Classes Owe, 49–50.

329. Discuss taxes on railroads.

Sidgwick, 574.   Leroy–Beaulieu, I., 542–545.

330. Discuss an export duty on raw cotton; on wheat.

Mill, V., 4, §6.   Sidgwick, 576.

331. How are we interested in the repeal of the Brazilian export duty on coffee?

332. Coal is essential to England's industry. It has been feared that her supply would be exhausted, and it has been proposed to put an export duty on it. Would that be wise?

Jevons, Coal Question, 260–261 ; 276–278 ; 354–360.
Fawcett, Free Trade, 163–4.

333. Write an essay on income tax, including progressive income tax.

Leroy-Beaulieu, I., 126–164 ; 422–470.

334. Write out the notes of a speech which you would make, if you were a member of Congress this winter, and it was proposed to abolish the duty on sugar.

335. Draw up a budget for the United States for the fiscal year 1883–4 on the basis of the expenditures of 1882–3, showing what taxes or other means of revenue you would employ to provide the required amount.

XII.

ECONOMIC POLICY:

Protectionism.

336. What is the English system of free trade? England levies taxes on some imported commodities. How is this fact to be understood when she claims to have adopted free trade?
Sumner, Protection, 10.

337. Discuss export duties on raw materials and fuel, prohibitions on the export of machinery, prohibitions on the emigration of laborers, bounties on the export of finished products, and taxes on the imports of commodities, in their relations to each other and as parts of a general system.
Adam Smith, II., 79–99; 120–122; 226–246.
Sumner, Protection, 31.

338. Are there are any economic advantages in being the first to take a wise or right course? Does a merchant or manufacturer argue well who says: "I must cheat or I shall be beaten by my rivals who cheat?" Can you illustrate your answer by industrial copartnerships or free trade?

If all men were honest, would honesty have commercial value?

Mongredien, Wealth, 209-212.

339. Mill says (p. 515): "Those are therefore in the right who maintain that taxes on imports are partly paid by foreigners; but they are mistaken when they say it is by the foreign producer." What foreigner is it who pays? and what is Mill's argument?

340. It is said that exigencies arise in the history of a country when it just needs a little help to lift it over a difficulty. Criticise that notion. It is said that a protective tariff is just what is needed to give the assistance. Assume the general notion to be true and criticise the special device here proposed.

Princeton Review, March, 1881, p. 247.

341. State any proposition which you think you can maintain about the relation between high or low wages and international competition.

Sumner, Protection, 22, 42 ; Argument, etc., 10.

342. In the United States employers say that they need protection because they have to pay high wages. Employees say that they want protection so as to make their wages high. In Germany employees say that they want protection because their wages are low. In each case "high" or "low" is taken with reference to English wages. Criticise these arguments separately and in relation to each other

Sumner, Argument, etc., 8, 9.

343. If a man goes into a store and finds a piece of cloth such as he wants, does it make any difference to him, in any point of view, whether the cloth was made across the street or across the ocean? What about the cloth alone makes a difference to him?

344. Show the inconsistency between laying heavy duties on commerce and dredging out harbors; between taxing commerce and subsidizing ships; between protecting manufacturing and giving land grants to railroads which make new land accessible.

Sumner, Protection, 14; Jackson, 183-4.

345. Show that, if the protectionists are right in laying taxes "to develop our resources," resources are calamities. Why was the discovery of a nickel deposit in the United States a misfortune, and why may we regret that a tin mine has just been discovered?

346. Show the fallacy of the protectionist argument that capital, which would otherwise be unemployed, is, by protection, drawn into use; that a higher organization of industry is brought about which increases production.

Sumner, Argument, etc., 5.

347. One country has a good and cheap government and therefore low taxes. Another country has a bad and very expensive government, and therefore high taxes. In the first, industry is very free and secure. In the second it is trammelled and uncertain. The former therefore beats the latter even in its own markets. The producers of the latter therefore demand a protective tax to "offset the heavier domestic taxes which they have to pay," and "to put them on an equality with their rivals." After such tax is laid, how many independent evils is the second country suffering from? .

348. Show the fallacy: "The money to replace what has been burned [at Chicago] will not be sent abroad to enrich foreign manufacturers, but, thanks to the wise policy of protection which has built up American industry, it will stimulate our own manufacturers, set our mills running

faster, and give employment to thousands of idle workmen." Was the fire a calamity?

Compare this case: When Pittsburg was burning in 1877, during a riot, the bystanders refused to put out the fire, saying: " Let her burn, boys! . It will make work."

Cairnes, Principles, 253.   Sumner, Argument, etc., 8.

349. A process having been discovered for utilizing as fuel great mountains of refuse which has hitherto accumulated at the mouth of coal mines, the production of steel rails is greatly cheapened for the mills which are near the coal mines. The competition of these mills closes up others less favorably situated. Is this course of things a calamity to anybody? If so, to whom? Is it not a misfortune and injustice to the owners and laborers in the mills which are closed that they are not allowed to set up a tariff wall around themselves?—Suppose that the cheapening of production had been accomplished in a foreign country and was not available here, and then answer the same questions.

350. " Upon what a narrow and stupid basis do they discuss this American system of industry! They speak of it as if it were protection of the mill owners, of the mine owners, of the proprietors and managers of furnaces and of railroads and of ships. Why, of course, they have their share in the workings of industry, but the object of it all, and the political reason of it all, is that we mean to protect our wages from being beaten down by the peasantry or the laborers of foreign countries, whose dignity, whose manhood, whose equality is not preserved."

351. "It is not enough to show that iron costs less in England than it costs here. The question is whether iron would not cost far more here, if this country, with its enormous demand, were dependent upon British manufacturers for iron." Discuss the argument that we ought to develop industries at home by protection in order not to be at the mercy of foreign monopolists.

352. "In the first place, I freely grant that the enhanced price of the protected articles represents a loss to the consumers, and through them to the nation. Against this loss I claim that the following gains, where they are gains, should be offset :

First—Any effect that protection may have on the " margin of cultivation."

Second—Any effect upon the equation of international demand.

Third—Any effect upon the employment of classes (women and children) who would not have found employment at all in unprotected industries.

Fourth—Any tendency that engaging in the protected industries may have in employing skilled in the place of common labor.

Fifth—Any tendency which protection may have to lead a nation to save rather than borrow the capital its industries call for.

Sixth—Any influence which protection may have upon the state of the arts and the progress of invention, both in the nation and in the world at large."

Examine these points.   Are there such gains? Can protective taxes win them?

Mill, III., 17, §5.

353. "We must remember that a worker may gain more by having his industry protected than he will lose by having to pay dearly for what he consumes. A system which raises prices all round—like that in the U. S. at present—is oppressive to consumers, but is most disadvantageous to those who consume without producing anything, and does little, if any, injury to those who produce more than they consume."

354. "Last year, notwithstanding the high duties, we imported of iron and steel, in their various forms, a million and a half tons. These required, for their production, twenty-eight million days' work, and if made in our country would have given steady employment at two dollars a day, to one hundred thousand men, for eleven months, and have left all the profits here, instead of in England."

355. "What I hope I have done is to show that 'capital' is subject to the law of supply and demand. There are many things which affect the rate at which accumulation will go on. Its ultimate amount, however, is always limited, at least as to circulating capital, by the number of laborers, and the average amount of capital that can be profitably utilized in employing them. When accumulations exceed this point one or more of three things may occur: 1. An increase of laborers. 2. Transferring some of them to industries in which it takes more capital per capita to keep laborers at work; or, 3, an accumulation occurs which depresses profits and causes an industrial stagnation.

Now, when protection diverts labor from agriculture to manufacturing it allows accumulation to go on to a point it could not otherwise reach, because it transfers labor to employments requiring more capital.

The yearly profits on such accumulations are a pure gain to the country, and a valid offset against the loss to the consumer, which is the only economic effect free traders seem able to comprehend."

356. Criticise the policy of commercial or reciprocity treaties.

Fawcett, Free Trade, Chap. 6.   Baden-Powell, 273–278.

357. The imports of the United States are not sufficient to give return cargos for the ships which are required to take out the exports. Therefore the steamers put in bunks for the westward passage and compete with each other for emigrants. Show how the tariff intensifies this relation of things. What, then, is the effect of the tariff on the net return for American wheat and cotton, on immigration, and therefore on the wages of American wage-receivers?

Cf. Jevons, Coal, 253 fg.

358. Describe the comparative results of free trade and protection in Victoria and New South Wales.

Baden-Powell, Chap. V.

359. The Duc de Broglie wrote a book to prove that under free trade the "less favored nations" would lose population and capital which would find better employment elsewhere. To counteract this he would not adopt the protective system, "nursing father of ignorance, laziness and routine," but would adopt freedom of commerce "under the reservation of the exceptions of which it admits and in the limitations which science sets for it, and with liberty to extend the limitations and exceptions according to national circumstances."—Criticise this proposition. If the whole population and capital of France should move to Greenland, what harm would it do to anybody?

360. "It might shake the Victorian protectionist's faith in his own doctrine if he would reflect that his most effectual protection against the foreigner would be the exhaustion of his own gold fields."—Why? Put American for Victorian, and wheat and cotton fields for gold fields. and say if the argument is equally strong.

Cairnes, Essays, 33–40.   Cairnes, Principles, 313–31b.

361. If a bounty is paid on exports, who pays it and who gets it?

Adam Smith, II., 79–86.   Fawcett, Free Trade, 16–28.

362. "With a perfectly free trade it would probably be impossible for any country to refrain from specializing, while the country that was economically strongest would certainly gain at the expense of others, as it would have an advantage in all the bargains of international trade." Show the fallacy of this passage. Define " economically strongest." Note "all the bargains."
Cunningham, 410.

363. "One land would manufacture and another produce raw materials, so that under a combined regime of perfect free trade no nation would be likely to consist permanently of a mingled population, of whom a large part were engaged in tillage and another large part were in manfacturing." Show, by a study of the distribution and differentiation of industry inside the United States, that this deduction is erroneous.
Cunningham, 410.

364. "A simple case will show how a duty may at once protect the native manufacturer adequately and recoup the country for the expense of protecting him. Suppose that a 5 per cent. duty is imposed on foreign silks, and that, in consequence, after a certain interval, half the silks consumed are the product of native industry, and

that the price of the whole has risen 2½ per cent. It is obvious that, under these circumstances, the other half which comes from abroad, yields the State 5 per cent., while the tax levied from the consumers on the whole is only 2½ per cent., so that the nation, in the aggregate, is at this time losing nothing by protection except the cost of collecting the tax, while a loss equivalent to the whole tax falls on the foreign producers."

Show that the above, if generalized, means as follows: criticise each of the assumptions, and the practicability of the device; note that it is given under the art of political economy:

(1) If a tax of n per cent. is wanted, but (2) if the tax in question may be used up to produce only $\frac{n}{m}$ of revenue, the rest being surrendered to protection, and if another tax may be used for the deficiency, and (3) if the decrease in the total consumption due to advance in price, be left out of account, and (4) if we assume that the price over the whole outside market may be depressed by the tax, and (5) if the loss and waste of years in bringing about the desired result be disregarded, and (6) if the practical impossibility of bringing about the supposed state of things be overlooked, and (7) if the incidence of the tax, variation in price, etc., be measured by the price before the tax was laid, without regard

to deterioration in quality after the tax is laid, then, if a tax of n per cent. causes $\frac{1}{m}$th of the product to be imported and the price to advance $\frac{n}{m}$, the foreigner will pay n per cent. on $\frac{1}{m}$th of the supply and the consumer will pay $\frac{n}{m}$ per cent. on the whole of it, which will be equal. The former will be revenue and the latter can be devoted to protection.

Show that, if all else were sound, this must be modified to read: The foreigner would pay part of the tax, and the domestic consumer might devote to protection a sum equal to that part of the tax which the foreigner pays.

Show the fallacy of the whole argument. If the foreigner lowers his price for the protected market, what is true of the goods which he sends into that market and of his profits on them? Does he really pay any of the tax? Show that the consumer pays revenue n per cent. on $\frac{1}{m}$ imported, and protection n per cent. on the part $m - \frac{1}{m}$ produced at home.

Sidgwick, 491–492.   London Economist, Dec. 1, 1883.

365. Mr. Ward says that we have now, by our science of sociology, attained to the matter and method of scientific education. Here, then, he thinks, dynamic sociology may begin ; *i. e.*, the State may take measures for the application of scientific education and thus move on with regular and uninterrupted steps to the improvement of society.—Criticise this opinion.

366. Show that the improvement of society depends most of all on an advancing standard of parenthood. If, then, we could direct our science of sociology to the object of highest importance, we should endeavor to determine the moral and physical elements of a good parent, and to establish criteria for measuring and defining those elements. If, then, the State were provided by science with these criteria, it would have to determine a standard or limit of good parenthood, and take measures to prevent the marriage of any persons who were below the standard.

Prove the steps of this reasoning. Show why the point of view is erroneous, and why the conception of sociology which is here employed is chimerical.